EYEWITNESS
NATURAL
DISASTERS

Buddhist statue
survives tsunami

Fire engine

Optical telescope
scans space
for asteroids

Doppler radar
dome

Track buckled
by giant wave

Hurricane-warning
flags

EYEWITNESS
NATURAL
DISASTERS

Written by
CLAIRE WATTS

Consultant
TREVOR DAY

Spirit of
Smallpox
carving

Planet Earth

Body casts,
Pompeii

Seismograph

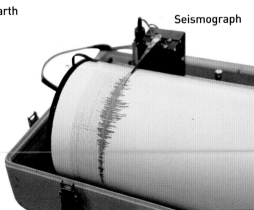

DK

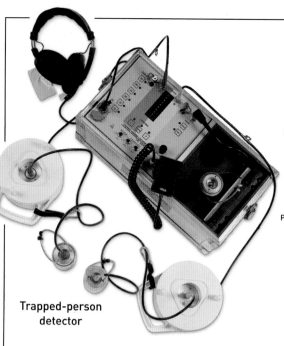

Trapped-person
detector

Project editors Jackie Fortey, Carey Scott
Designers Johnny Pau, Samantha Richiardi
Senior editor Rob Houston
Senior art editors Owen Peyton-Jones, Philip Letsu
Production editor Adam Stoneham
Publishing managers Caroline Buckingham,
Andrew Macintyre, Laura Buller
Managing editor Camilla Hallinan
Managing art editor Sophia M. Tampakopoulos
Production controller Rebecca Short,
Gordana Simakovic
Picture researchers Celia Dearing, Julia Harris-Voss,
and Jo Walton
DK picture library Rose Horridge
DTP designer Andy Hilliard
Jacket designer Sarah Ponder

FIRST REVISED EDITION
Consultant John Woodward

RELAUNCH EDITION (DK UK)
Senior editor Chris Hawkes
Senior art editor Spencer Holbrook
US senior editor Margaret Parrish
Jacket editor Claire Gell
Jacket designer Laura Brim
Jacket design development manager Sophia MTT
Producer, pre-production Nikoleta Parasaki
Producer Vivienne Yong
Managing editor Linda Esposito
Managing art editor Philip Letsu
Publisher Andrew Macintyre
Publishing director Jonathan Metcalf
Associate publishing director Liz Wheeler
Design director Stuart Jackman

RELAUNCH EDITION (DK INDIA)
Senior editor Bharti Bedi
Project art editor Nishesh Batnagar
Editorial team Sheryl Sadana, Virien Chopra
DTP designer Pawan Kumar
Senior DTP designer Harish Aggarwal
Picture researcher Nishwan Rasool
Jacket designer Dhirendra Singh
Managing jackets editor Saloni Talwar
Pre-production manager Balwant Singh
Managing editor Kingshuk Ghoshal
Managing art editor Govind Mittal

First American Edition, 2006
This edition published in the United States in 2015 by DK Publishing
345 Hudson Street, New York, New York 10014

Copyright © 2006, 2012, 2015 Dorling Kindersley Limited
A Penguin Random House Company

15 16 17 18 19 10 9 8 7 6 5 4 3 2 1
001—280099—Sep/15

A catalog record for this book is available from the Library of Congress.

ISBN 978-1-4654-3808-9 (Paperback)
ISBN 978-1-4654-3809-6 (ALB)

DK books are available at special discounts when
purchased in bulk for sales promotions, premiums,
fund-raising, or educational use. For details, contact:
DK Publishing Special Markets, 345 Hudson Street,
New York, New York 10014 or SpecialSales@dk.com.

Printed and bound in China

A WORLD OF IDEAS:
SEE ALL THERE IS TO KNOW
www.dk.com

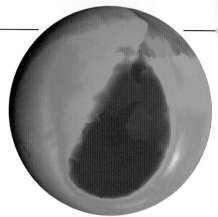

Ozone hole over
Antarctica

Tsunami warning buoy

Smoke jumper

Mayan rain god

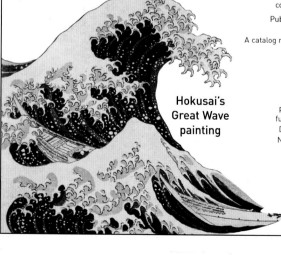

Hokusai's
Great Wave
painting

Contents

Lava fountains erupt
from Mount Etna

Dynamic planet	6		Raging waters	46
Restless Earth	8		Drought	48
The Earth shakes	10		Wildfire	50
Surviving a quake	12		Fighting fires	52
What is a tsunami?	14		Climate change	54
Wave power	16		Exploitation	56
Walls of water	18		Infectious diseases	58
Japan's terror	20		Epidemic	60
Recovery begins	22		The future	62
Warnings	24		Did you know?	64
Volcanoes	26		Timeline	66
Rivers of fire	28		Find out more	69
Avalanches and landslides	30		Glossary	70
Atmosphere	32		Index	72
Wild weather	34			
Hurricanes	36			
Battling winds	38			
Hurricane Katrina	40			
Twisting tornadoes	42			
Flood alert	44			

Dynamic planet

Planet Earth provides us with the air, food, materials, and warmth that we need to thrive. But it also generates catastrophes, from tsunamis to tornadoes, that damage the environment and property, and take and disrupt lives. Such disasters may be sudden and violent, like an earthquake, or gradual, like a drought. There are more than 700 natural disasters every year, affecting about one person in 30.

Tsunami strikes Lisbon
This picture of the 1755 earthquake and tsunami that destroyed Lisbon, Portugal, shows buildings leaning at impossible angles. Before instant media and photography, facts and images were often exaggerated.

Restless planet
Energy from the Sun drives Earth's weather, and is the source of such disasters as droughts, floods, and hurricanes. Heat from within Earth causes rock movement beneath us, which can lead to earthquakes, volcanoes, and tsunamis.

Land heaved upward, leaving this house at a precarious angle

Rivers of lava
Kilauea, Hawaii, is one of the most active volcanoes in the world, erupting almost constantly. There are more than 1,000 active volcanoes on land today that spew out fiery lava due to the high temperature and pressure deep underground.

Devastating earthquakes
Earthquakes are one of the most feared natural disasters. This street in Ojiya City, northern Japan, was destroyed following a quake in October 2004. In the 20th century, quakes killed almost 1.5 million people. In October 2005, a single quake killed 38,000 in Pakistan. Earthquake survivors are often left with nothing, as homes, farms, and offices are destroyed, and transportation links, electricity, water supplies, and telephone links are cut. Essential services, such as hospitals, may not be able to operate.

Blazing forests

Wildfires, such as this one that struck Big Sur, California, may be ignited by lightning or by a dropped match. They can destroy forests, leaving a scarred landscape, but forests have a natural ability to regenerate slowly. Sometimes, wind blows the fire toward an urban area, putting buildings and lives at risk from the flames and choking smoke.

New growth as first rainfall germinates seeds

A dry world

As the world's population grows, so does the demand for water. Human activities, such as cutting down forests, change local weather patterns, making droughts more likely. More than 100 million people suffer the effects of drought.

Piercing mouthparts for drawing blood

Deadly diseases

Most diseases that cause widespread illness and death are from microscopic organisms, such as the malaria-carrying parasite that lives in mosquito saliva. Malaria kills more than one million people every year, and 40 percent of the world's population live in high-risk malaria areas.

Residents carry their possessions as they flee the dangers of the erupting volcano

Escape

In 1984, scientists predicted the Mayon volcano's eruption in the Philippines, and so 73,000 people were evacuated. Modern technology, such as satellites that help produce weather forecasts, often makes it possible to predict disasters, giving people time to prepare and flee.

Restless Earth

Diamond embedded in volcanic rock

Deep inside Earth, the heat and pressure are so great they can turn carbon deposits into hard diamond. Earth's surface (crust) is divided into big slabs called tectonic plates. Some of these crunch together, others drift apart, and some grind past each other. The heat and pressure inside Earth disturb the tectonic plates. When this pressure is released at the planet's surface, it can cause earthquakes, volcanoes, and tsunamis.

South America and Africa fitted together

Atlantic Ocean now separates South America and Africa

Pangaea
Earth's tectonic plates formed 3.6 billion years ago. They constantly move and change shape, pushing continents together and apart. About 200 million years ago, at the time of the dinosaurs, all continents were part of one landmass—Pangaea.

Earth today
Over the last 200 million years, the tectonic plates between Europe and the Americas have moved apart, opening up the Atlantic Ocean. Each year, the continents shift by about half an inch (1 cm). The map will look different again in the future.

Earth's layers
Earth's land surface is made of continental crust 45 miles (70 km) thick. The seabed lies on oceanic crust 5 miles (8 km) thick. The entire crust floats on hot, solid mantle. Earth's metal core reaches 10,800°F (6,000°C).

Continental crust · Upper mantle · Lower mantle · Outer core · Inner core · Oceanic crust · African plate

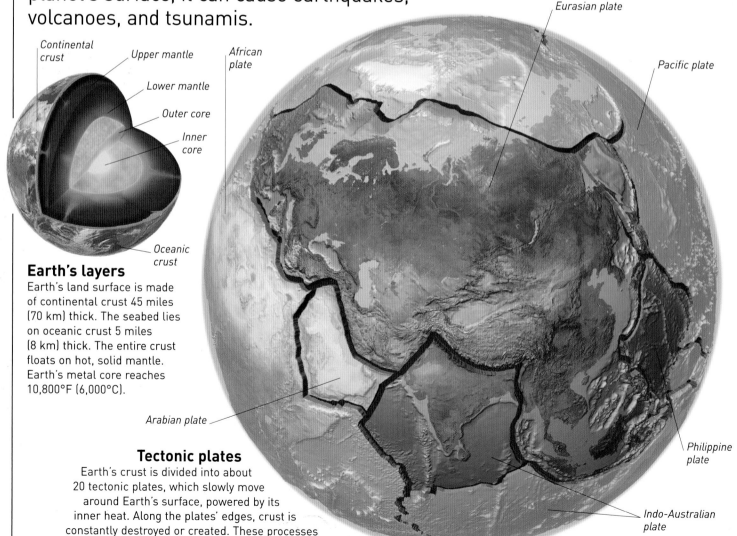

Eurasian plate · Pacific plate · Philippine plate · Indo-Australian plate · Arabian plate

Tectonic plates
Earth's crust is divided into about 20 tectonic plates, which slowly move around Earth's surface, powered by its inner heat. Along the plates' edges, crust is constantly destroyed or created. These processes cause most of Earth's earthquakes and volcanoes.

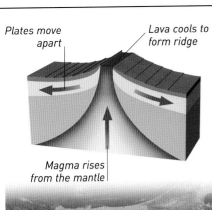

Plates move apart

Lava cools to form ridge

Magma rises from the mantle

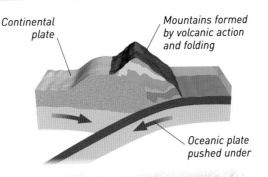

Continental plate

Mountains formed by volcanic action and folding

Oceanic plate pushed under

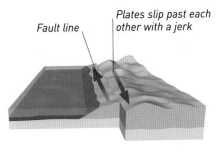

Fault line

Plates slip past each other with a jerk

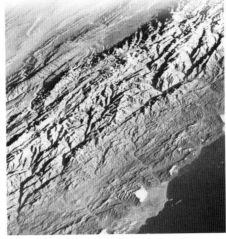

Divergent boundary

When plates move apart, or diverge, magma (called lava once it reaches the surface) rises into the gap to form new crust. In the Red Sea, the African and Arabian plates have been diverging for 50 million years. In oceans, most diverging plates form ocean ridges.

Convergent boundary

When an oceanic plate moves toward, or converges with, a continental plate, the oceanic plate is pushed beneath the continental plate, creating a trench in the ocean floor, and melts into magma. This rises through the continental crust to form a volcanic mountain range, such as the Andes in South America.

Transform fault

Where two plates slide past each other, a transform fault occurs, such as the San Andreas Fault in California. Friction between the rocks may make the plates jam. Pressure makes them jerk past each other, causing an earthquake or tsunami.

New crust

Wherever magma (molten rock) emerges from Earth's mantle, new crust is created. This may happen in a violent volcanic eruption or as the plates diverge. Magma also leaks through weak points in Earth's crust at hot spots far from the plate boundaries. As the plate moves over the hot spot, the magma may form a chain of volcanic islands, such as the Hawaiian islands.

Steam rises as hot lava from Kilauea volcano, Hawaii, flows into the sea

As lava cools it hardens into rock

The Earth shakes

Earth's plates are always moving. Sometimes, they jolt, making the ground shake. Devised in 1935, Charles Richter's scale is usually used to measure earthquakes; the smallest measure up to 3.5 (enough to rattle a cup on a table), and the most severe measure over 8 (enough to destroy cities). Earthquakes cannot be prevented, but scientists can forecast some by studying past records and the buildup of stresses in rocks.

Poseidon the Earth Shaker
In ancient Greece, people believed that earthquakes were caused by the god of the sea, Poseidon. When he was angry, Poseidon stamped on the ground or struck Earth with his three-pronged trident, setting off an earthquake. His unpredictable, violent behavior earned Poseidon the name Earth Shaker.

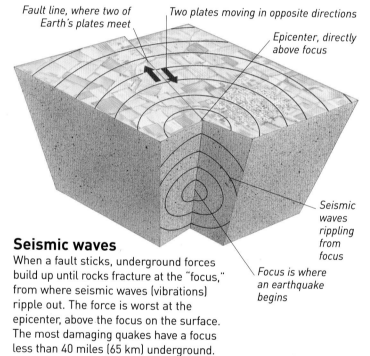

Fault line, where two of Earth's plates meet

Two plates moving in opposite directions

Epicenter, directly above focus

Seismic waves rippling from focus

Focus is where an earthquake begins

Seismic waves
When a fault sticks, underground forces build up until rocks fracture at the "focus," from where seismic waves (vibrations) ripple out. The force is worst at the epicenter, above the focus on the surface. The most damaging quakes have a focus less than 40 miles (65 km) underground.

San Andreas Fault
The 750-mile- (1,207-km-) long San Andreas fault line in California splits the Pacific and North American plates, and generates earthquakes. Some parts slip regularly, producing slight tremors; others get jammed and shift as pressure is released, causing a major earthquake.

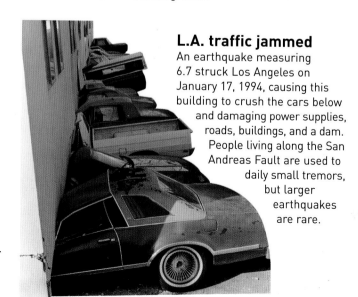

L.A. traffic jammed
An earthquake measuring 6.7 struck Los Angeles on January 17, 1994, causing this building to crush the cars below and damaging power supplies, roads, buildings, and a dam. People living along the San Andreas Fault are used to daily small tremors, but larger earthquakes are rare.

Haiti quake

An earthquake measuring 7 hit Haiti in the Caribbean on January 12, 2010. The island had no building code standards; 250,000 houses and 30,000 commercial structures were destroyed, and 100,000 people died, crushed by collapsing buildings. Rescue efforts were hampered by communication failure and 54 aftershocks.

Earthquake detector

In 132 CE, Chinese astronomer Zhang Heng invented the first seismoscope for detecting ground movement. It shows the direction a tremor comes from within a range of about 40 miles (65 km).

Earth tremors cause one of the dragons to release a ball

Colored bands are narrow around the epicenter, showing greater land displacement

Epicenter of earthquake

Ball falls into open mouth of toad below

Toad farthest from epicenter catches the ball. The quake lies in the opposite direction from the toad.

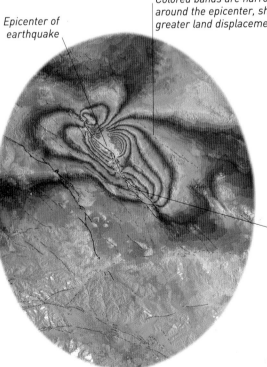

Fault line

Fine needle moves with tremors, recording the vibrations with ink

The greater the shockwave, the wider the zigzag on the display

Ground movements

This satellite radar image shows land movement following a quake measuring 7.1 in California in 1999. The colored bands show where people felt the same quake intensity, and where ground displacement occurred.

Revealing quakes

Earth tremors can be detected, recorded, and measured by a seismograph, which detects foreshocks produced by deep rocks fracturing before an earthquake. Monitoring foreshocks helps predict earthquakes.

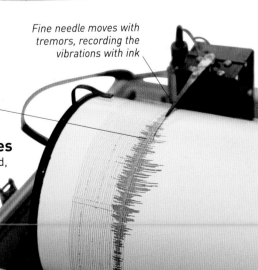

Surviving a quake

Earthquakes have little impact in the wilderness, but can devastate built-up areas. In some earthquake zones, specially constructed buildings absorb vibrations without collapsing, but even they can fall down in a major earthquake. When an earthquake strikes, emergency plans are put into action: trained teams rescue the injured, fight fires, evacuate danger zones, make ruined buildings safe, and restore essential services.

Fighting fire
When the ground stops shaking, damage to electrical equipment and gas pipes can lead to an outbreak of fires. Firefighters have to struggle through ruined buildings and broken roads to reach the blaze. After the 1995 earthquake in Kobe, Japan, many of the ancient wooden buildings burnt down when firefighters ran out of water.

City in ruins
The ancient fortress, or citadel, of Arg-e Bam stood on a hill overlooking the city of Bam in Iran for 11 centuries, until December 27, 2003. A violent earthquake flattened the mud-brick fortress, the city of Bam, and other historic buildings. More than 26,000 people died and 70,000 were left homeless.

The Citadel Of Arg-e Bam before 2003 earthquake

The Citadel Of Arg-e Bam after 2004 earthquake

Shaking caused the loose ground to move like a liquid, and it could no longer support the highway

Shock in Japan
On January 17, 1995, an earthquake measuring 6.9 struck the city of Kobe, Japan. Road bridges collapsed as the bolts holding them together snapped. Much of Kobe is built on land that becomes unstable during an earthquake, and the epicenter of the 1995 earthquake was only 12 miles (20 km) from the city; shockwaves damaged 140,000 buildings and killed 5,500 people.

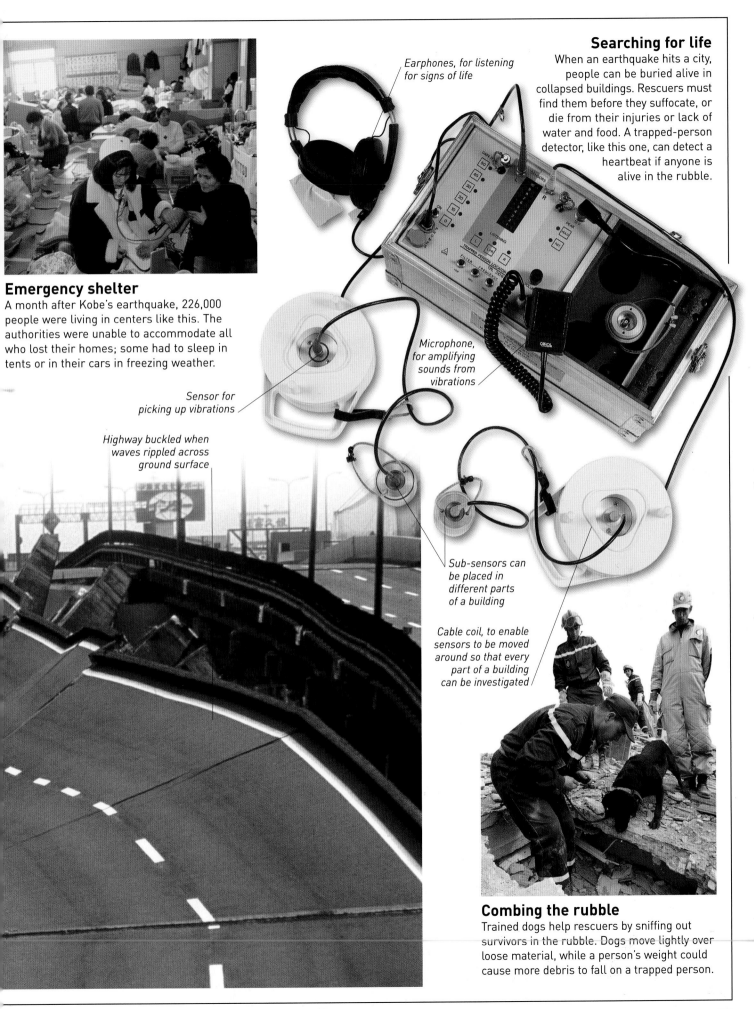

Earphones, for listening
for signs of life

Searching for life

When an earthquake hits a city,
people can be buried alive in
collapsed buildings. Rescuers must
find them before they suffocate, or
die from their injuries or lack of
water and food. A trapped-person
detector, like this one, can detect a
heartbeat if anyone is
alive in the rubble.

Emergency shelter

A month after Kobe's earthquake, 226,000
people were living in centers like this. The
authorities were unable to accommodate all
who lost their homes; some had to sleep in
tents or in their cars in freezing weather.

Microphone,
for amplifying
sounds from
vibrations

Sensor for
picking up vibrations

Highway buckled when
waves rippled across
ground surface

Sub-sensors can
be placed in
different parts
of a building

Cable coil, to enable
sensors to be moved
around so that every
part of a building
can be investigated

Combing the rubble

Trained dogs help rescuers by sniffing out
survivors in the rubble. Dogs move lightly over
loose material, while a person's weight could
cause more debris to fall on a trapped person.

What is a tsunami?

The first sign of a tsunami (soo-nah-mee) approaching the coast may be a sudden swell in the ocean. Tsunamis are caused by huge volumes of water shifting, usually due to undersea earthquakes. Traveling at speeds of up to 600 mph (950 kph), a tsunami can be a chain of waves hitting the shore at heights of 100 ft (30 m). Walls of water can slam against the coast for hours, stripping it of sand and vegetation and sweep inland, flooding everything in their path.

The great wave
This Japanese painting by Katsushika Hokusai shows a towering wave. Tsunamis were called tidal waves, but now that we know they are not caused by tides, we call them by their Japanese name, which means harbor wave.

Landslide
Tsunamis can be caused by landslides into the sea. As debris plunges into the water, the sudden shifting of water can generate a tsunami. However, tsunamis started by landslides usually affect only the local area and quickly subside.

Soufrière Hills volcano, Monserrat, 1997

Clouds of smoke and ash cascading from Mount Pelée, Martinique

Volcanic eruption
When Mount Pelée, Martinique, erupted on May 7, 1902, a torrent of volcanic gas, ash, and rock fragments, called a pyroclastic flow, fell into the sea. It caused a tsunami that destroyed the harbor.

Impact from space
Every day, hundreds of rocks fall from space. Most burn up in the atmosphere to become shooting stars. Those that reach Earth are called meteorites. If a huge object—such as an asteroid—hits the ocean, its impact may cause a tsunami.

Meteorite composed of stone and iron

Earthquake
Most tsunamis are caused by earthquakes around Earth's tectonic plates. Huge cracks in the ground can open up, as here in Gujarat, India. When this occurs under the ocean, tsunamis can occur.

Satellite image of a section of the coastline of Sumatra before the tsunami of December 26, 2004

After the tsunami

One of the worst natural disasters of the early 21st century began with an earthquake measuring 9 on the seafloor 150 miles (240 km) off the coast of Sumatra in the Indian Ocean. The resulting tsunami traveled 2,800 miles (4,500 km) in just seven hours. It killed more than 200,000, and stripped bare all low-lying areas, covering them with mud. Sand and rock were swept away from beaches; the sea was full of mud and debris.

Mud and debris cover the beaches

Vegetation stripped away, exposing rock and soil

Tsunami grows higher, reaching up to 100 ft (30 m) before it breaks

Decreasing depth causes the waves to slow down

Waves, about 3 ft (1 m) high, ripple outward from the disturbance

Giant ripples produced by shifting of water

Crack in ocean floor created by earthquake

Direction of fault movement

From earthquake to tsunami

When an earthquake causes a shift in the seabed, the displaced water creates giant waves that move vast distances at great speed. Near the shore, shallow depths make them slow down and grow higher until they break on land.

Wave power

Tsunamis caused by earthquakes and volcanoes (tectonic tsunamis) can travel huge distances across oceans. Local tsunamis, caused by landslides, can cause higher waves, but do not travel as far. If both tectonic and local tsunamis occur, it can be devastating. The biggest tsunamis are caused by asteroid impacts. But it is not just the tsunami's origin that affects its power; the shape of the coastline also plays a role.

Harbor wave
On November 18, 1867, an earthquake measuring 7.5 created a tsunami that struck the steamship *La Plata* in St. Thomas's harbor in the Virgin Islands. Eyewitnesses described a wall of water 20 ft (6 m) high sweeping over the island's harbor.

A breaking wave can generate a force equivalent to the thrust of a space rocket's main engines

Rock face stripped of vegetation by the tsunami is still bare 14 years later

The biggest tsunami
On July 9, 1958, an earthquake measuring 8.3 saw 90 million tons of rock crash into Lituya Bay, Alaska. A 1,700-ft- (525-m-) high splash stripped vegetation, leaving bare rock. A rock slide then created a 100-ft- (30-m-) high local tsunami—the largest in recent history.

Sea sculpture

The extraordinary towers and caves of Cathedral Rocks, New South Wales, Australia, were cut from the cliffs and gouged out in just a few minutes by a tsunami thousands of years ago. Scientists believe the rocks were sculpted by one of the most powerful types of tsunamis—one caused by an asteroid hitting the ocean or a landslide on the seabed.

Oil tanker hurled around by tsunami

Burning waters

On Good Friday, March 1964, an earthquake off the Alaska coast caused landslides that created a 30-ft (9-m) local tsunami in the town of Seward. Oil-storage tanks along the bay were damaged and ignited. Twenty minutes later, the first 40-ft (12-m) wave of a tectonic tsunami spread flaming oil into Seward, setting it on fire.

Tsunamis and tidal bores

When a tsunami-generated wave reaches a river mouth or a bay, the shape of the land funnels the wave into a narrow, high wall of seawater weighing billions of tons. Unusually, high tides create similar walls of water, called bores, as seen here on the Qiantang River, eastern China, where 30-ft (9-m) bores have moved at 25 mph (40 kph).

Walls of water

The earthquake that triggered the Indian Ocean tsunami of December 26, 2004, released energy equal to that of thousands of nuclear weapons. Ocean waves radiated out from its epicenter, close to the island of Sumatra, Indonesia; the strongest traveled east and west. Bangladesh, to the north, had few casualties; Somalia, far to the west, was harder hit. Some waves bent around landmasses to hit the western coasts of Sri Lanka and India.

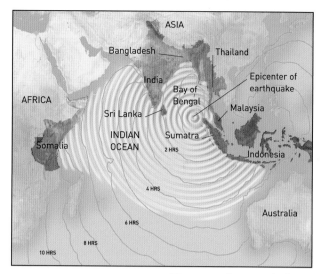

Tsunami travel time
Shock waves spread out from the epicenter like ripples from a stone dropped in water. Each pink line on the map indicates one hour of travel time. The waves took 15 minutes to reach the nearest land—Sumatra—seven hours to reach Somalia, and six hours to wreak minor damage in northern Australia.

Seismogram
This seismograph reading shows the earthquake that shook southern Asia just before 8 a.m., local time. Most earthquakes last a few seconds; this went on for 10 minutes. No one realized that it had triggered a tsunami.

Before a tsunami, the sea can recede by as much as 1.5 miles (2.5 km) on gently sloping shores

The calm before the strike
Up to half an hour before the tsunami struck, the ocean appeared to drain from beaches. When the trough—a wave's low part—reaches shore, it sucks water offshore, called drawback. Many people went to investigate the exposed sand, with tragic results.

Tide flooding Sri Lanka
This photograph, taken from a beachside resort's hotel room in southwest Sri Lanka, shows when 33-ft- (10-m-) high waves rushed in like a very strong, fast tide, two hours after the earthquake, and kept coming.

Banda Aceh

The place most devastated by the tsunami was the Indonesian city of Banda Aceh, on the island of Sumatra. The city was just 155 miles (250 km) from the earthquake's epicenter and, when the waves receded, it lay in ruins. One hundred thousand people may have lost their lives in the Banda province in just 15 minutes.

Buildings utterly flattened

Wrecked boats, India

Livelihoods as well as lives were lost in the tsunami. All around the Indian Ocean, fishing boats lay battered beyond repair on the shore, like these in the south Indian state of Tamil Nadu. The tsunami destroyed two-thirds of its fishing fleet.

Twisted track

Near Seenigama, on the southwestern coast of Sri Lanka, 1,500 passengers perished when the tsunami hit the train in which they were traveling. The waves swept the engine and cars from the track, and forced up the rails themselves, leaving a mass of twisted wood, metal, and tangled debris.

Japan's terror

The tsunami that struck Japan on March 11, 2011, was one of the most catastrophic on record. Huge waves reached heights of 133 ft (40.5 m), destroying everything in their path. Thousands died as the debris-loaded water surged inland, flattening coastal cities, wrecking road and rail links, plus a nuclear power plant that released radiation and may take decades to clean up.

Earth shock
The biggest earthquake ever recorded in Japan shook the ocean floor 43 miles (70 km) off Honshu, the main Japanese island, and triggered the catastrophic tsunami. This building in Onagawa was destroyed by the earthquake and tsunami.

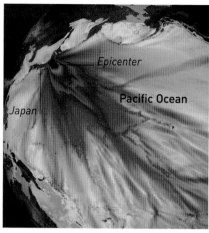

Radiating waves
On the ocean floor off Japan, one part of Earth's crust is pushing beneath another. In March 2011, the boundary between the two gave way, raising the seabed by 23 ft (7 m) and creating huge waves that moved across the Pacific. The dark colors on this map show the highest waves; the red and orange, the smaller ones.

Surging water
When the tsunami reached shallow water, its waves slowed down and rose far higher than thought possible, overwhelming the tsunami-resistant sea defenses, as seen here at the fishing port of Miyako. Here, the sea rose to at least 28 ft (8.5 m) above normal high-tide level, lifting cars over the sea wall and ripping boats from their moorings.

Nuclear crisis

At the Fukushima nuclear power plant on the east coast of Japan, the nuclear reactors shut down automatically after the earthquake. They still generated heat, but this was dealt with by an emergency cooling system. When the tsunami hit 50 minutes later, it swept over the 19-ft (5.8-m) sea wall, destroying the emergency cooling pumps and causing the reactors to overheat.

Desperate rescue

When the giant waves finally stopped, survivors and rescue workers combed through the wreckage for trapped victims. This young girl was rescued from Kesennuma, a fishing port north of the earthquake's epicenter that suffered the earthquake, tsunami, and fires.

Meltdown

As the crippled nuclear reactors at Fukushima got hotter, the radioactive fuel rods that generate heat melted in three of the six reactors, creating pools of dangerous radioactive molten metal. Three reactor buildings were wrecked by explosions, as seen here, and stored fuel rods in water tanks also overheated, threatening more radioactive leaks. All people living within 19 miles (30 km) were evacuated.

Debris piled up by the tsunami waves

Innocent victims

The earthquake and tsunami killed more than 18,000 people—90 percent of them drowned by the raging floodwaters. Many more were left homeless, including at least 100,000 children. Here, a shocked survivor gazes at the destruction in Ishinomaki, where one school lost 74 of its 108 students.

Recovery begins

Following a tsunami disaster, aid comes from around the globe. The first task is to provide shelter and medical care. Then, the debris left by the water must be cleared, as well as victims' bodies before they start to rot and spread disease. Once the clearing tasks are over, people can get back to normal life. But recovery can be slow, with vital infrastructure destroyed and people suffering from shock and grief.

Health check
A child is checked for radiation exposure in Fukushima, Japan, after the 2011 tsunami damaged Fukushima's nuclear reactors, and dangerous amounts of radiation leaked out. Local people were evacuated, but will need health checks for many years to come.

In memory
This Buddhist statue was left on the beach at Khao Lak, Thailand, in memory of those killed in the 2004 Asian tsunami. Religious services were held all along the coast.

Refugee camp at Bang Muang, Phang Tha, in Thailand

Elephant handler wears mask as protection against the smell of decaying bodies

Tent city
Vast camps housed people who were made homeless by the 2004 Asian tsunami. Poor sanitation in huge refugee camps can lead to outbreaks of diseases such as cholera and typhoid. This was prevented by health services, which provided safe drinking water and food, the means to cook, and adequate sanitation.

Elephants at work
After the 2004 Asian tsunami, corpses had to be buried quickly to prevent outbreaks of disease. Thailand's elephants were able to reach otherwise inaccessible areas. First, dogs sniffed out bodies, then the elephants nudged aside building ruins or fallen trees to reveal the corpses beneath. They also moved the bodies to burial sites.

Clearing the damage
Rescuers search for missing residents in Miyagi prefecture, four days after the March 11, 2011, earthquake and tsunami. Japan's government asked people not to panic-buy food and supplies in the aftermath.

Temporary shelter for aid workers and their equipment

Boat building
On coasts hit by the 2004 Asian tsunami, local people had to rebuild boats that had been damaged by the waves. Boats are vital to the region's fishing industry, but many tourist resorts also use them to show visitors the coral reefs.

Boat building on the beach at Phuket, Thailand

Back to school
These children at an elementary school in Natori, northern Japan, lost many of their friends when the school was flooded during the 2011 Japanese tsunami. Many were also made homeless when their houses were swept away.

Warnings

Tsunami evacuation sign

In 2004, the Asian tsunami struck the Indian Ocean out of the blue. In the Pacific, there was a tsunami warning system. Oceanographers monitored the ocean for possible tsunamis, and used sirens and broadcasts to warn people. In 2006, a similar program was set up in the Indian Ocean, but all such systems are limited. The earthquake that triggered the 2011 tsunami was so close to Japan that people on the coast had little time to escape.

Observation

A sensor on the seabed below this Japanese buoy measures water pressure. If a tsunami passes over it, the water pressure changes and the sensor alerts the buoy, which sends a signal to Japan's Tsunami Early Warning Center via a satellite.

Antenna for sending signals to satellite

Solar panels power the buoy

Holding back the waves

This enormous floodgate in Nomazu Port, Japan, has a door 30 ft (9.3 m) high, which automatically shuts if a seismograph senses an earthquake that could lead to a tsunami. Most of Japan's population lives along the coast, so measures like this offer vital protection to the region's earthquake-prone cities.

Gate raised to allow tall ships into the harbor

Massive gate weighs 840 tons

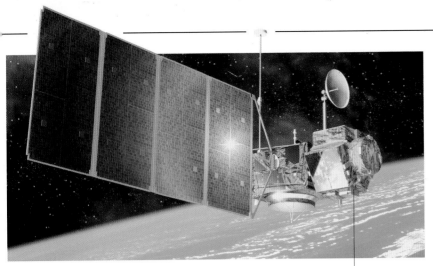

The sea from space

Launched in 1992, the Poseidon satellite records sea surface height and ocean currents from its orbit above Earth. Tiny changes in sea level after an undersea earthquake can give advance warning of a tsunami.

Two radar altimeters measure sea surface height

Tsunami Warning Tower

When the Warning Center spots an impending tsunami, it races to spread the news to affected coasts. New warning towers, like this one in Thailand, are being built around the Indian Ocean. They have sirens, and antennae that can interrupt TV and radio broadcasts to send text messages that advise people to move to higher ground, away from the coast.

Tsunami Warning Center

The Pacific Tsunami Warning Center, Hawaii, gathers data about undersea earthquakes and sea level changes to see if a tsunami is likely. They can predict where and when a tsunami will arrive within half an hour of an earthquake. A similar warning system was put in place around the Indian Ocean in 2006.

Sonar device

The first step for a tsunami warning system is to monitor earthquake activity on the seabed. This sonar device will map the Indian Ocean seabed near Banda Aceh, where the 2004 tsunami originated. It reflects sound off the seabed to build a 3-D image.

Tourists relax in front of the Tsunami Warning Tower at Phuket, Thailand

Land areas above sea level

Steep slope leading to ocean depths

Areas below sea level are blue/green

The ocean floor in 3-D

Sonar maps like this 3-D image of the seabed around California enable oceanographers to study the ocean-floor's contours. Regular scanning shows seabed movement, such as shifts along a fault line, which could signal tsunami-triggering events.

Volcanoes

Pockets of hot molten (liquid) rock called magma float underneath Earth's solid crust. Magma rises to the surface through weak spots in the crust—most of which lie on the margins of Earth's tectonic plates. As magma pushes up, pressure builds until magma breaks through Earth's crust, sending rock, ash, and lava crashing onto the surface as a volcano.

Sleeping volcano
Japan's Mount Fuji last erupted in 1707 and is now dormant—it shows no sign of activity, but may erupt in the future. Active volcanoes frequently erupt. Volcanoes that have been dormant for thousands of years are called extinct—but they may erupt again.

Goddess Pele
Legend says that the Hawaiian goddess of volcanoes, Pele, has a volcano's powers to melt rocks, destroy forests, make mountains, and build new islands.

Ashy steam blasting from the volcano's vent

Fiery river
When magma inside a volcano is runny and does not contain much gas, it erupts in a hot stream of lava, like this in Hawaii. When the magma is thick and sticky, it traps gases, such as steam and carbon dioxide, inside it. Sticky, viscous magma erupts in a violent explosion of lava globules and burning ash.

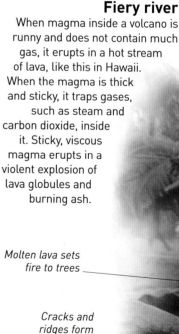

Molten lava sets fire to trees

Cracks and ridges form as the lava sheet hardens

Birth of an island
Most volcanic eruptions occur under the oceans. In 1963, an eruption near Iceland made the sea steam, as seawater poured into the volcano's vent and was boiled by its heat. Over a few years, volcanic lava and ash piled up into a small island—Surtsey.

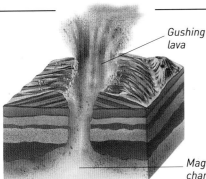

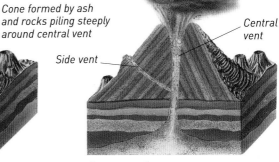

Shield cone volcano

Runny lava erupts from the vent in a gushing river, or fountain. This runny lava spreads over a wide area. Later eruptions form a mountain with gently sloping sides. A typical shield cone volcano is Mauna Kea, Hawaii.

Gushing lava

Magma chamber

Cinder cone volcano

These volcanoes usually have one vent that erupts ash and rocks that fall in a ring. The straight-sided cone is formed from erupted rocks. Cinder cones, such as Paricutin, Mexico, are rarely over 1,000 ft (300 m) above land.

Single vent (opening)

Cone formed by ash and rocks piling steeply around central vent

Stratovolcano

Thick, sticky lava cools and hardens quickly to produce a steep mountain. Rocky, ashy eruptions alternate with lava, creating layers in the cone- or dome-shaped mountain, which may grow 10,000 ft (3,050 m) high.

Side vent

Central vent

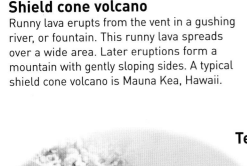

Temperature taking

Volcanologists (volcano scientists) measure the ground temperature around volcanic vents to find out what is going on beneath Earth's surface. Active volcanoes are monitored frequently, so that people can be warned if the ground temperature rises and an eruption is likely.

Taking samples

After eruptions, volcanologists in heat-protective suits collect fresh lava samples. These samples can show changes in a volcano's behavior. For example, different gas mixtures may make it more explosive.

Rivers of fire

An exploding volcano is a magnificent sight, as enormous pressures force lava, ash, rocks, and superheated gases out of Earth. After an eruption, soil may be nourished with mineral-rich volcanic ash, which is good for farming. Today, eruptions can be predicted and people can be evacuated from the danger zone. However, a major eruption can affect weather around the world.

Plume of volcanic ash

Mount St. Helens

When Mount St. Helens, Washington, erupted on May 18, 1980, so much rock was blown off its top that it lost 1,312 ft (400 m) in height. A cloud of ash spread over 20,000 sq miles (50,000 sq km), causing a major hazard for aircraft. In 2010, a similar ash cloud was spewed out by the Eyjafjallajökull volcano in Iceland. It caused most European countries to halt air traffic in their airspaces.

Jets of fire

In 2001, Italy's 11,120-ft- (3,390-m-) high Mount Etna exploded with a bang. Etna is one of Europe's highest mountains and its most active volcano. Usually, it erupts in small, continuous bursts. Lava flows constantly damage roads and property, and threaten towns. Concrete barriers, trenches, even explosives, have been used to try to redirect the lava, with limited success.

After the eruption

The Mount St. Helens eruption flattened around 230 sq miles (600 sq km) of forest, and wiped out local wildlife. Scientists estimate that it will take 200 years for the forest to return to its pre-eruption condition.

Fern

Lichen

Moss

New life

The first plants to appear in solidified lava after an eruption are mosses, lichens, and weeds. Volcanic rock may take decades to become fertile soil for larger plants to take root.

Pyroclastic flow
On June 15, 1991, Mount Pinatubo, in the Philippines began erupting after lying dormant for 600 years. Rock particles and ash flew 25 miles (40 km) into the atmosphere. This deadly cloud of hot gas and debris, called a pyroclastic flow, hurtled at speeds of 100 mph (160 kph) across the surrounding area.

Deadly dust
As ash from Mount Pinatubo filled the air with a choking cloud and covered the fields, farmers took buffalo to look for unaffected areas. Many developed pneumonia from inhaling the gritty ash, and entire harvests were lost.

Panic in Pompeii
The prosperous Roman town of Pompeii lay in the shadow of Italy's Mount Vesuvius, which had been dormant for centuries. Townsfolk were therefore surprised when it erupted on August 24, 79 CE. This re-creation shows the pyroclastic flow about to engulf the town.

Ash around the bodies hardened, preserving the shapes of the dead

Buried town
Many people managed to escape from Pompeii, but some 2,000 were trapped in the town. They died of suffocation as a choking pyroclastic flow swept through the streets. Pompeii and its dead were buried under 100 ft (30 m) of ash; no remains were discovered until excavations began in 1860.

Fluid lava pours down Mount Etna's slopes

Avalanches and landslides

St. Bernard rescue dog

When gravity's pull is greater than the forces that hold rock and snow together on a steep hillside, the rock and snow may crash down the slope. Unstable rocks and soil can cause a landslide, while snow can hurtle as an avalanche, burying anything in its path. Speedy rescue is essential to save buried survivors; for hundreds of years, rescue dogs have helped find trapped people.

Avalanche warning sign
In mountain ski resorts, warning signs indicate avalanche risk. It is difficult to predict exactly when and where an avalanche will occur, but experts can tell when the snow layers become unstable enough to trigger an avalanche.

To the rescue
High in the mountains, rescue teams use helicopters to reach injured people quickly. A winch is used to lower rescuers and haul up the injured on stretchers. The pilot must be careful because even the noise and draft of a helicopter can trigger another avalanche.

Torrent of snow
When mountain snow builds into an unstable overhang, or thaws and becomes loose, an earth tremor or loud noise can cause an avalanche. As it rushes down the slope, the avalanche loosens more snow and picks up rocks and soil. It can be half a mile (800 m) wide. Anyone caught in it has a 5 percent chance of survival.

Avalanche prevention
Fences built across slopes can stop tumbling snow before it grows into a huge avalanche. Sometimes, explosives are used to trigger small avalanches. This prevents the buildup of too much snow, which could cause a major avalanche.

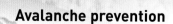

Landslide types

There are four types of landslide. Soil creep is when there are slow, tiny shifts in the soil particles. Slumping is a faster slide, when slabs of land slip down a slope. Debris flow happens when a slope becomes saturated with water, triggering a landslide of water-soaked soil and rocks. Rockfalls are sudden slides caused by heavy rain or frost dislodging larger rock pieces.

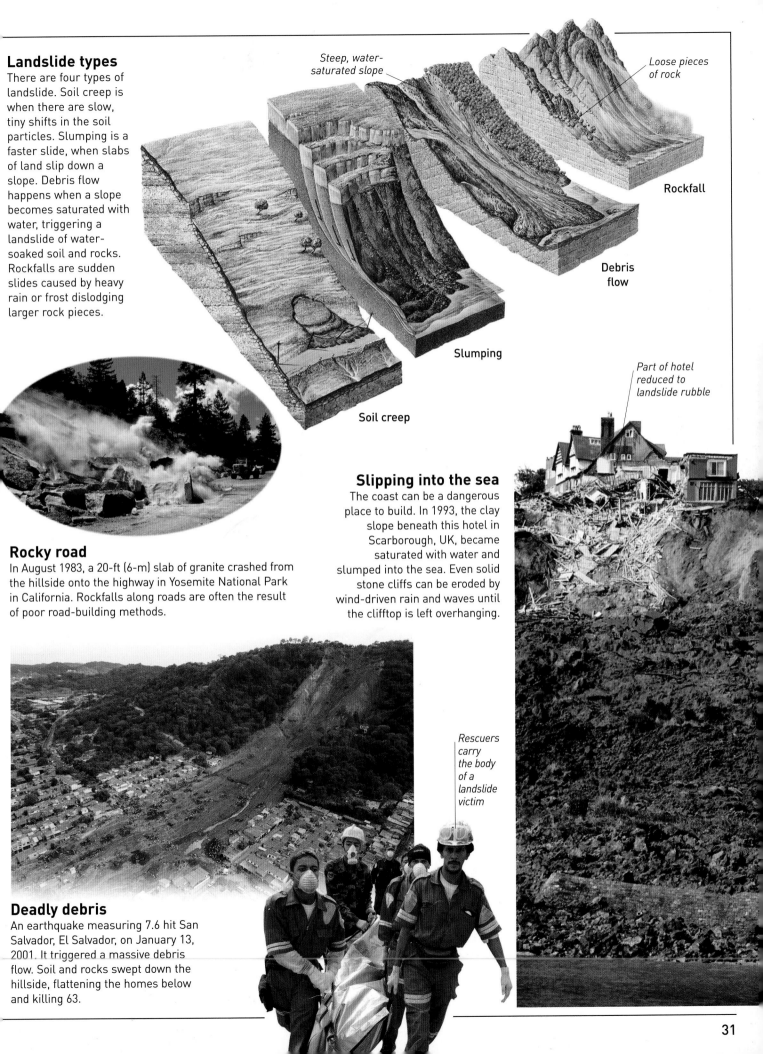

Steep, water-saturated slope

Loose pieces of rock

Rockfall

Debris flow

Slumping

Soil creep

Rocky road

In August 1983, a 20-ft (6-m) slab of granite crashed from the hillside onto the highway in Yosemite National Park in California. Rockfalls along roads are often the result of poor road-building methods.

Slipping into the sea

The coast can be a dangerous place to build. In 1993, the clay slope beneath this hotel in Scarborough, UK, became saturated with water and slumped into the sea. Even solid stone cliffs can be eroded by wind-driven rain and waves until the clifftop is left overhanging.

Part of hotel reduced to landslide rubble

Rescuers carry the body of a landslide victim

Deadly debris

An earthquake measuring 7.6 hit San Salvador, El Salvador, on January 13, 2001. It triggered a massive debris flow. Soil and rocks swept down the hillside, flattening the homes below and killing 63.

Atmosphere layers
The atmosphere is made up of four layers, based on temperature and humidity (the amount of water in the air). The outer layer, the thermosphere, extends into space. Gravity keeps water and air in the lowest layer, the troposphere. The Sun's rays warm the air and water, causing them to move, making the weather.

Some satellites orbit at the top of the thermosphere

Aurora, the Northern and Southern Lights, occur in the lower thermosphere

4. Thermosphere thins out into space about 400 miles (650 km) above Earth's surface

Most meteors burn up before they reach the mesosphere

3. Mesosphere extends 50 miles (80 km) above Earth's surface

2. Stratosphere reaches up to 30 miles (48 km) above Earth's surface. It contains ozone, which absorbs some of the Sun's ultraviolet radiation.

1. Troposphere extends 12 miles (19 km) above Earth's surface. The weather happens here.

Atmosphere

The atmosphere is a band of gases—mostly nitrogen, oxygen, and argon—held around Earth by gravity. Air masses move around the atmosphere, creating Earth's weather. A region's pattern of weather over time is called the climate. In some areas, extreme weather is part of the climate; in other places, where the climate is less severe, people are totally unprepared for natural disasters.

Thunderclouds in the atmosphere
Viewed from space, the atmosphere looks like a light haze around Earth. In the troposphere, thunderclouds are silhouettes against the orange sun. The sky's blue is caused by sunlight interacting with gases in the air. The blue sky's layers in this picture were due to volcanic ash from Mount Pinatubo, Philippines, and Mount Spurr, Alaska.

Soaring clouds
Clouds form in the low layer of the troposphere. Cumulonimbus storm clouds like this one can reach 15 miles (24 km) high, and punch through the top of the troposphere. Large storm clouds can hold 275,000 tons of water and produce thunderstorms, hailstorms, tornadoes, torrential rain, and snow.

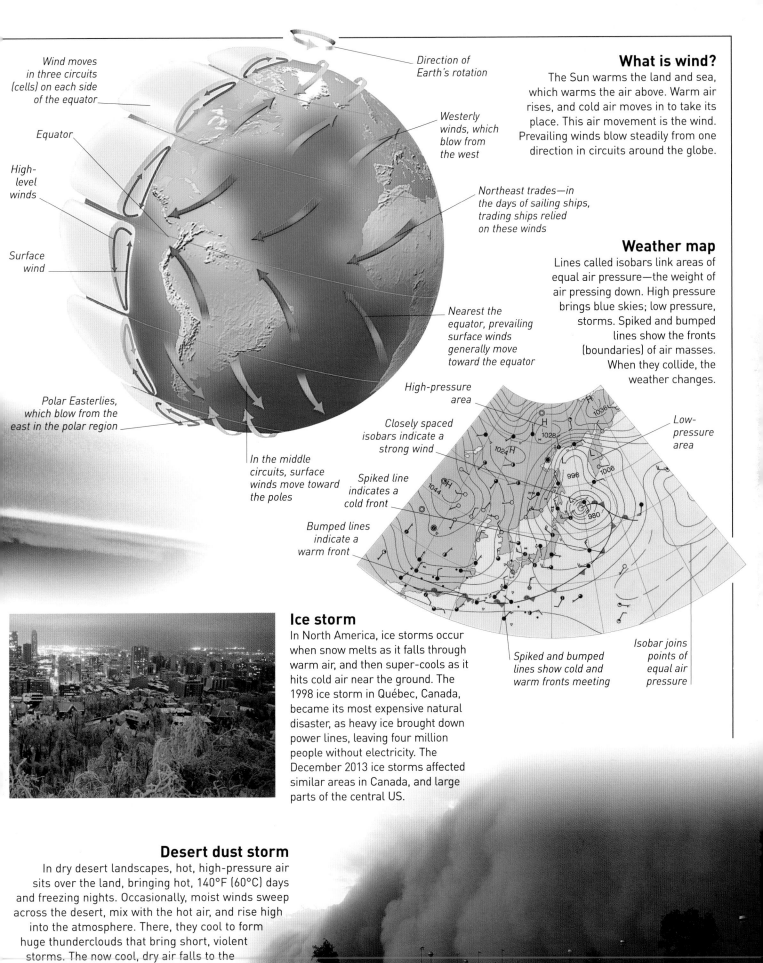

Wind moves in three circuits (cells) on each side of the equator

Direction of Earth's rotation

Equator

High-level winds

Surface wind

Westerly winds, which blow from the west

Northeast trades—in the days of sailing ships, trading ships relied on these winds

Polar Easterlies, which blow from the east in the polar region

Nearest the equator, prevailing surface winds generally move toward the equator

In the middle circuits, surface winds move toward the poles

What is wind?

The Sun warms the land and sea, which warms the air above. Warm air rises, and cold air moves in to take its place. This air movement is the wind. Prevailing winds blow steadily from one direction in circuits around the globe.

Weather map

Lines called isobars link areas of equal air pressure—the weight of air pressing down. High pressure brings blue skies; low pressure, storms. Spiked and bumped lines show the fronts (boundaries) of air masses. When they collide, the weather changes.

High-pressure area

Closely spaced isobars indicate a strong wind

Spiked line indicates a cold front

Bumped lines indicate a warm front

Low-pressure area

Spiked and bumped lines show cold and warm fronts meeting

Isobar joins points of equal air pressure

Ice storm

In North America, ice storms occur when snow melts as it falls through warm air, and then super-cools as it hits cold air near the ground. The 1998 ice storm in Québec, Canada, became its most expensive natural disaster, as heavy ice brought down power lines, leaving four million people without electricity. The December 2013 ice storms affected similar areas in Canada, and large parts of the central US.

Desert dust storm

In dry desert landscapes, hot, high-pressure air sits over the land, bringing hot, 140°F (60°C) days and freezing nights. Occasionally, moist winds sweep across the desert, mix with the hot air, and rise high into the atmosphere. There, they cool to form huge thunderclouds that bring short, violent storms. The now cool, dry air falls to the ground and spreads out, creating 60-mph (100-kph) winds, which whip up dusty soil into a dust storm.

Wild weather

At any time, 2,000 thunderstorms light up the sky around the world. A bolt of lightning can reach 54,000°F (30,000°C), five times hotter than the Sun's surface, and its electrical charge can kill instantly. Most thunderstorms are in summer, when warm air rises to form thunderclouds. These storms can bring torrential rain or hail. Their paths are tracked using satellites, weather stations, and weather planes.

Eiffel Tower struck
Like other tall buildings, the Eiffel Tower in Paris, France, is protected from lightning damage by a lightning conductor—a metal cable that leads the electrical charge to the ground, where it discharges harmlessly.

Thunder and lightning
Inside a storm cloud, water droplets and ice crystals rise and fall, building up a static electrical charge that sends a spark of lightning to the ground (fork lightning), or among the clouds (sheet lightning). The air around it heats up and expands, creating a shock wave, heard as thunder.

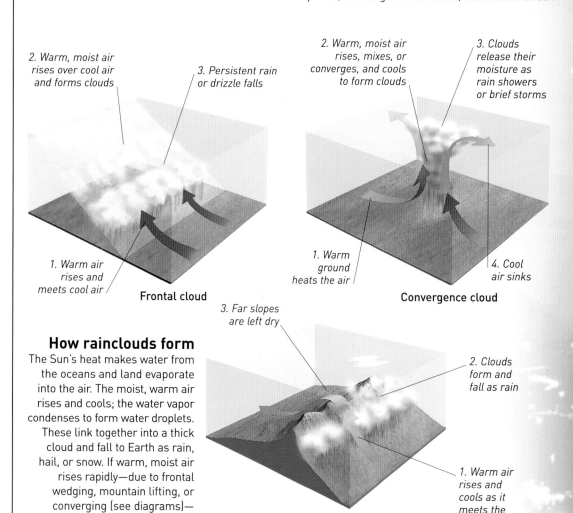

2. Warm, moist air rises over cool air and forms clouds

3. Persistent rain or drizzle falls

1. Warm air rises and meets cool air

Frontal cloud

2. Warm, moist air rises, mixes, or converges, and cools to form clouds

3. Clouds release their moisture as rain showers or brief storms

1. Warm ground heats the air

4. Cool air sinks

Convergence cloud

3. Far slopes are left dry

2. Clouds form and fall as rain

1. Warm air rises and cools as it meets the mountain

Mountain lifting

How rainclouds form
The Sun's heat makes water from the oceans and land evaporate into the air. The moist, warm air rises and cools; the water vapor condenses to form water droplets. These link together into a thick cloud and fall to Earth as rain, hail, or snow. If warm, moist air rises rapidly—due to frontal wedging, mountain lifting, or converging (see diagrams)—storm clouds occur.

Flying into the storm

Airplanes such as this WC-130 Hercules monitor weather. When severe weather is expected, such planes can fly into the storm to analyze the wind speed, strength, and direction. This data can help predict which areas will be struck by the storm, and how badly.

Radar equipment in the plane's nose

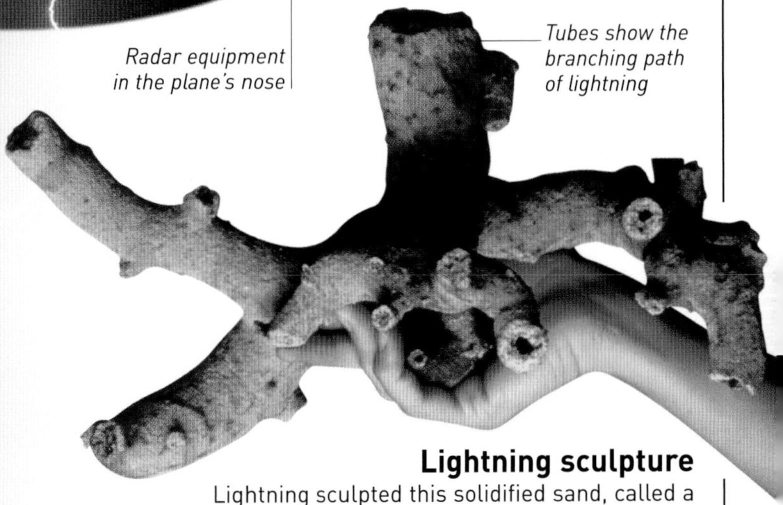

Tubes show the branching path of lightning

Lightning sculpture

Lightning sculpted this solidified sand, called a fulgurite. As lightning passed through the sand, it heated up the grains to melting point and fused them together into hollow tubes. Lightning's heat can set trees and wooden buildings on fire.

Thunderclouds over Gillette, Wyoming

Black clouds and hail

Hailstones form when raindrops, moving up and down in freezing black thunderclouds, become coated with ice. Hailstones can be larger than baseballs but most are pea-sized. Even tiny balls of ice can damage crops and property and turn roads into ice rinks.

Giant hailstone

Baseball

Hurricanes

In late summer, above tropical seas along the equator, huge rotating storms develop. The storms—called hurricanes when they start over the Atlantic Ocean, cyclones in the Indian Ocean, and typhoons in the Pacific Ocean—can be 300–500 miles (500–800 km) across and travel great distances. High winds, torrential rain, and surges of seawater leave a trail of destruction as they sweep inland.

Storm at sea

Dark threat

Tropical storms are fueled by the Sun's heat evaporating ocean water, which rises with the warm air to build vast storm clouds. The lifting air creates a zone of low atmospheric pressure. The surrounding air then rushes into the low-pressure zone, driving howling winds.

Hurricane forming

This satellite image from September 2004 shows spiraling clouds forming Hurricane Ivan over the Atlantic Ocean. For a hurricane to form, seawater must be above 80°F (27°C), fueling winds of up to 73 mph (118 kph). A hurricane can pick up two billion tons of water vapor from the sea a day, to be dumped on land as potential rain.

Dry air sinks into the eye of the storm

Air spirals inward at the bottom of the hurricane

The fastest winds and heaviest rain spiral around the low-pressure eye wall

Sea surface bulges in the low-pressure eye area

Red arrows show spiraling bands of wind and rain

Blue arrows show cool air spiraling outward at the top of the hurricane

Inside a hurricane

A hurricane forms when an area of warm air rises above the ocean and sucks in surrounding air. Earth's rotation makes the air spin. The spinning air rises, cools, and creates a spiral of storm clouds. A hurricane's eye is an area of calm air at its center.

The calm eye of the storm

Thick clouds spiral around the eye

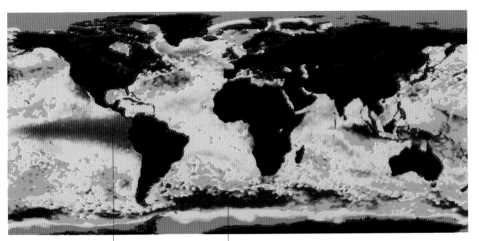

El Niño

Every three to seven years, a weather pattern called El Niño causes winds over the Pacific to change direction. This colored satellite image shows sea temperature changes due to the 1997 El Niño event. Winds push warm water to South America, bringing tropical storms, while areas west of the ocean may suffer drought.

Red shows sea temperatures farthest above normal

Purple shows sea temperatures farthest below normal

Eye of the storm

Hurricane Fran's fiercest wind and most torrential rain batter a gas station in North Carolina in 1996. The most violent part of the hurricane often follows a calm period—the sky may suddenly clear and the air grow still, as the eye of the storm passes. A few moments later, the storm returns with renewed vigor.

Hurricane warnings

Flags like these alert residents and ships when a hurricane is nearing the coast. Weather forecasters broadcast a "weather watch" on television, radio, and the Internet, telling people to look out for updates. Once certain the storm will strike, they issue a severe weather warning. It is best to shelter in a brick or concrete building, away from windows.

Wind and waves

In 1998, Hurricane Georges sent huge waves crashing onto the shore of Florida. When the eye passes over the coast, it brings a deadly wall of water, called a storm surge, up to 10 ft (3 m) high, caused by the eye's low air pressure.

Palm trees bend but rarely break in hurricane winds

3. Andrew over the Gulf of Mexico, August 25

2. Andrew passing over Florida, August 24

1. Hurricane Andrew at sea, August 23, 1992

Battling winds

Every year, about 90 hurricanes batter the world's coasts. Their wind speed and air pressure are measured to try and predict how they will develop. Satellites can spot hurricanes as they form, but accurate data comes from planes, known as hurricane hunters, sent into the hurricane. When it moves over land, a hurricane slowly runs out of energy; if it sweeps out to sea, warmth from the water can speed up the wind once more.

Hurricane hunters

In 1999, during a 12-hour flight into Hurricane Floyd, hurricane hunters recorded wind speed, humidity, and pressure. Weather-station computers used the data to predict Floyd's path, although hurricanes can change direction.

This infrared satellite image of Hurricane Floyd helped the hurricane hunters plan their flight

Capsized yachts

Hurricane Andrew tore through Florida in August 1992. A storm surge 17 ft (5.2 m) high left yachts in Key Biscayne's marina in a heap. The storm weakened as it crossed Florida, but grew strong again over the Gulf of Mexico's warm waters.

Hurricane Andrew

This sequence of satellite images shows Hurricane Andrew's path as it moved east to west. Continuous wind speeds of 142 mph (228 kph) with 199 mph (321 kph) gusts were measured before the measuring devices were destroyed. Andrew killed 26 people; it narrowly missed Miami, where many more lives could have been lost.

Wooden building, easily destroyed by a hurricane

Great storm of '87

In the middle of an October night in 1987, a severe storm hit southern Britain. As it brewed out in the Atlantic, the storm mixed with warm winds from a hurricane. As a result, some gusts of wind reached hurricane speeds of 122 mph (196 kph), toppling 15 million trees and ruining buildings.

Trees uprooted by the force of the wind

Cyclone Nargis

The tropical cyclone that hit Myanmar (Burma) on May 2, 2008, was the worst natural disaster in Burma's recorded history. A 13-ft (4-m) storm surge swept inland across the low-lying Irrawaddy Delta; the destructive flood waters killed 138,000 people.

Houseboat tipped over by massive waves

Path of Georges, 1998

These men struggled against the 89-mph (144-kph) winds to reach a solid building as Hurricane Georges tore across Florida. By the time the storm reached the US, it had ravaged the Caribbean, killing more than 600 and ruining most of the crops.

Hurricane Katrina

Hurricane Katrina hit the Gulf Coast in August 2005, leaving a million people homeless, five million without power, and over 1,800 dead in the country's most destructive and costly natural disaster. Historic New Orleans lay under many feet of water; evacuees went to makeshift emergency shelters in the city and in nearby states, or moved in with relatives. Many said they were unlikely to return to the disaster-struck region.

Course of Katrina

Hurricane Katrina hit the Bahamas, south Florida, Louisiana, Mississippi, and Alabama between August 23–31, 2005. Winds reached a maximum windspeed of 170 mph (273 kph) and 200 miles (320 km) of coastline suffered a storm surge. The wind finally began to lose strength 150 miles (240 km) inland, near Jackson, Mississippi.

Storm surge

As the hurricane's eye moved across the Mississippi coast, it created a storm surge almost 33 ft (10 m) high. In the town of Long Beach, cars and rubble were swept into a towering heap against a building.

Sousaphone is too valuable to leave behind

Leaving home

On August 28, Hurricane Katrina was heading for New Orleans; its mayor ordered an evacuation. With no electricity, clean water, or food supplies, the last of those able to evacuate left, bringing a few belongings.

Underwater city

Rising floodwaters breached levees (embankments) designed to protect New Orleans from flooding. One day after Katrina hit, 80 percent of the city was flooded, some areas by 20 ft (6 m) of water. It took several weeks to repair the levees and pump out the water.

Broken windows

Curtains dangle outside hotel windows smashed by the force of Hurricane Katrina. Beds were seen flying out of the windows of one hotel. However, some modern buildings like this one survived relatively unscathed. Many of the city's famous wooden buildings, particularly those in the historic French Quarter, were largely spared, as the area did not suffer as much flooding as other parts of New Orleans. A commission was set up to advise the government on how best to rebuild, taking into account the needs of all citizens.

Boat rescue

Thousands of New Orleans residents were left behind when the hurricane struck. Many of them gathered in evacuation centers to await rescue. After the storm, rescuers arrived in boats to pick up the people who were stranded and conducted a house-to-house search to check for other survivors.

Clear eye of the storm

Strong eyewall winds

A solitary car travels toward the city as most residents rush to leave

Fleeing Hurricane Rita

Three weeks after Katrina, hurricane warnings of Rita sent residents of cities like Houston, Texas, rushing to evacuate, causing accidents on jammed roads. The mass evacuation likely saved many lives.

Twisting tornadoes

The most violent winds on Earth, tornadoes (nicknamed twisters) can travel across land at speeds of 125 mph (200 kph). They can hurl around objects as large as trains, and rip roofs off houses. Tornadoes have hit almost every state in the US, but most of the world's tornadoes occur in the American Midwest's open prairies, where tornado season runs from May to October.

Flying fish
Tornadoes passing over lakes and oceans may suck up fish and frogs, then drop them on dry land.

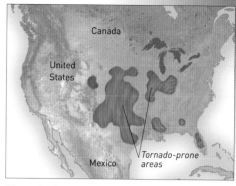

North America's Tornado Alley
Tornado Alley, in the center of the US, covers parts of Kansas, Oklahoma, and Missouri—the Great Plains; 80 percent of Earth's tornadoes occur here. In summer, cold air from Canada underrides warm, moist air from the Gulf of Mexico and hot, dry air from the Plains, causing atmospheric instability.

Tower of cloud called a thunderhead tops the supercell

Revolving mesocyclone sucks up dust from the ground

Storm clouds
Strong winds moving in different directions in a huge, dark storm cloud (supercell) create low pressure beneath the cloud. Warm, moist air rushes into the updraft to meet cold air higher up. The two air masses turn around each other to form a wide air column—a mesocyclone.

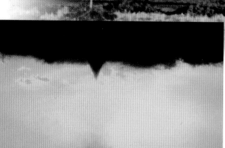
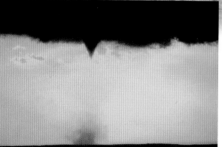
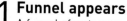

1 Funnel appears
A funnel of water vapor extends down from the cloud. As warm, moist air from the atmosphere is sucked into the mesocyclone's base, it spins upward, carrying dust with it.

2 Column forms
Warm air rises and cools, forming water vapor that joins the swirling funnel. When it touches the ground, sucking up more dust, it becomes a tornado and is clearly visible.

3 Dying down
Most tornadoes last about three minutes; the tornado slows down as it runs out of moist, warm air at the bottom or when cool, dry air sinks from the cloud.

Terrifying twister

Inside the tornado's column, air whirls inward and upward, creating a flow called a vortex, at up to 300 mph (500 kph). Low pressure inside the vortex makes the twister suck up items beneath it, like a vacuum cleaner. Tornadoes travel about 6 miles (10 km) before they run out of energy, but one twister may trigger another, leading to a tornado outbreak.

Wind speed is faster in narrow parts of the column

Dust devil

As air rises in the hot desert, it can create a draft that begins to swirl, just like a tornado, picking up dust and sand. Called dust devils, they can reach 1.2 miles (2 km) high. They are less fierce than tornadoes, with winds reaching up to 60 mph (100 kph).

Tornado damage

After a tornado, the surrounding area is often flattened, with vehicles crushed by falling debris or smashed by the twister, trees snapped in two, and power lines trailing from broken poles. Flimsy mobile homes are particularly at risk from tornado damage.

Storm chasers

Scientists known as storm chasers follow severe storms to monitor their progress. A Doppler radar mounted on a truck allows them to watch for a vortex developing inside the storm clouds. But even they cannot predict a tornado more than 24 hours in advance.

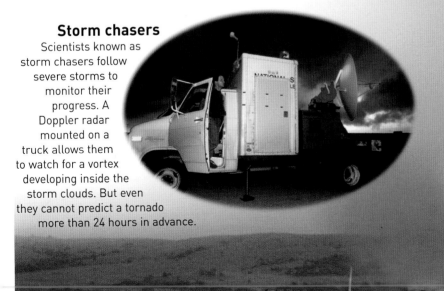

Waterspout

A tornado over the sea or a lake contains a column of condensed water, forming a waterspout. The wind speeds in a waterspout are usually less than those in a tornado, but the vortex could still lift a boat out of the water.

Flood alert

Water is vital to survival, but huge storm waves from the sea and flooding rivers make water a deadly enemy. Floods can sweep away people, animals, and poorly constructed buildings, and damage century-old buildings and valuable artworks. In steep landscapes, torrential rain can cause a flash flood—a surge of water that rises so rapidly it can catch people unprepared.

Rainy season
In India, children celebrate monsoon season, which starts with a thunderstorm and week-long torrential rain. Even though it brings floods, the monsoon is welcomed, as it ends the hot, humid season, and provides water for crops.

Flood plains of Lower Nile River

Fertile flood plains
Ancient Egyptians relied on the Nile's annual flooding, which naturally fertilized the flood plain (the land either side of a river). Since 1970, the Aswan High Dam has reduced flooding; today's farmers use fertilizers instead.

Flooded farmhouses at Machland, Austria, August 2002

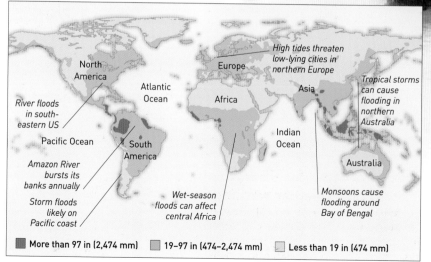

Inland flooding
In 2002, torrential rain in central Europe and failing flood defenses saw rivers flood in the Czech Republic, Austria, and Germany. In the Czech capital, Prague, water filled the underground rail system. River floods in urban areas can turn towns into lakes, and cause flash floods from water rushing downhill.

Map showing the annual amount of rainfall around the world

North America

Atlantic Ocean

Europe

High tides threaten low-lying cities in northern Europe

Asia

Africa

Tropical storms can cause flooding in northern Australia

River floods in south-eastern US

Pacific Ocean

South America

Indian Ocean

Amazon River bursts its banks annually

Australia

Storm floods likely on Pacific coast

Wet-season floods can affect central Africa

Monsoons cause flooding around Bay of Bengal

■ More than 97 in (2,474 mm)   ■ 19–97 in (474–2,474 mm)   ■ Less than 19 in (474 mm)

The world's rainfall
The average global rainfall is 40 in (1,000 mm) a year. But this is not evenly dispersed. The amount of rain an area gets depends on factors such as air temperature, land shape and size, and the season.

Melting glacier
The slow melting of frozen river ice or mountain glaciers cannot cause a flood, but floating chunks of melting ice can form a dam across the river, causing an overflow upstream. When the ice dam cracks, the released water causes a flash flood.

Pond formed by melted ice (meltwater)

Diverting the waters
Levels of some rivers are constantly monitored, and "sluices" channel water away from flood-prone areas. When sluice gates are open, excess water gushes into a runoff lake.

Sluice gates on Three Gorges Dam, Hubei Province, China

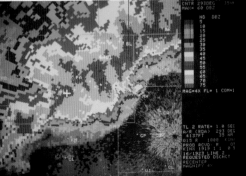

Protecting London
Tidal rivers, such as the Thames, are at risk from storm surges and floods due to unusually high tides. The Thames Barrier's gates close to prevent tidal surges from traveling upriver, protecting London.

Gates open to let river traffic through

Doppler radar dome receives returning radio waves

Red areas show approaching storm

Color codings for storm magnitude

Severe weather warnings
Doppler radar equipment makes accurate weather forecasts. It locates storms and measures their speed and direction by bouncing radio waves off clouds. This Doppler readout shows a storm in Kansas.

Raging waters

When a flood strikes, roads become impassable. With no way to escape the flood, people climb higher as the waters rise, onto roofs or in high trees, and wait for rescue helicopters or boats. One way to protect people from flooding is to stop building settlements on flood plains, but many large cities have already been built on them. In heavily populated, low-lying countries, such as Bangladesh and the Netherlands, there is not enough higher ground.

Noah's ark
In the Bible story, Noah's ark floated on a flood caused by 40 days of heavy rains. Noah and his passengers stayed on the ark for a year.

Ball of smoking incense

The right rain
Rain has always been vital for crops, and storms destructive. The Mayans hoped Chac, their god of rain, would provide rain but keep floods at bay.

The usual course of the Yangtze River

Houses under 3 ft (1 m) of water

Controlling the Yangtze River
China's Yangtze River used to flood regularly after heavy rain, killing thousands in some years. One of the worst floods, in August 2002, displaced 900,000 people. In 1994, the Chinese government had begun work on the Three Gorges Dam (the world's largest dam) to control the flooding. It was completed in 2006, but has caused other problems, such as earth tremors.

Road to nowhere
In 1993, the US's Midwest region had 10 times the usual amount of rain. The Mississippi and its tributary, the Missouri, flooded 31,000 sq miles (80,000 sq km) of land, including this bridge in Quincy, Illinois.

Aerial view of swamped cars near Wangaratta, Australia

Swirling waters
In southeastern Australia, cars sit in floodwater after heavy rain in September 2010. The state of Victoria suffered its worst floods in a decade, forcing cities to evacuate and cutting the electricity to 40,000 homes. Within three months, more floods devastated the state of Queensland.

Container for emergency food ration

Living with floods
Bangladeshis, used to the annual monsoon floods from the huge Ganges and Brahmaputra rivers, line up for supplies. But in 1997–1998, the El Niño weather pattern triggered so much monsoon rain that two-thirds of the country was flooded. Ten million people lost their homes.

Drought

It is hard to tell when a drought starts, but a drought is well underway when rivers run dry. It may cause a famine, and people and animals starve. The best preparation is to store water when it is plentiful, but the driest places never have enough water. In such places, drought cannot be prevented—but famine can, as long as water, food, and aid reach people in time.

Vanishing sea

The Aral Sea between Kazakhstan and Uzbekistan shrunk by 90 percent by 2007, and is still shrinking, despite efforts to save the small northern section. It has become more salty, too, killing the fish that lived there.

Boat grounded on sands that were once under the Aral Sea

Underground water

During a drought, soil and surface water dry up, but groundwater flows deep underground, trapped by hard layers of rock. Deep wells tap into this. In 2003, Gujarat in India suffered its worst drought in 10 years. People traveled far to deep wells, often on foot, and waited their turn to get water.

Field of dried-out sunflowers in Spain

Thirsty crops

In a drought, crops such as these sunflowers die, and the farmers suffer losses. In wealthy countries, hosepipe bans may occur, but there is usually enough water in reservoirs for drinking and washing until rain replenishes water supplies.

Holding back the desert

During droughts, sand dunes can spread, burying nearby towns and farms. To stop this, farmers plant millet crops in the dunes to bind the sand together and stop it from blowing to the fields.

Dust Bowl

In the 1930s, intensive farming ruined the soil in the US Great Plains. When drought struck, the soil turned to dust and blew away. Crop failures and famine followed. Half a million people abandoned their farms.

Burial mounds

Brick lining stops soil from collapsing into the well

Metal pots lowered on ropes to reach groundwater

Animal carcass, a common sight during severe droughts

Famine

When drought hit Ethiopia and Sudan in 1984–1985, crops failed, and then livestock starved. As a result, the people had no food and no income to buy any, and they too starved. In the famine that followed, 450,000 died.

Refugee camp

In the worst droughts, people have to gather in refugee camps, like this one in Mogadishu, Somalia, to receive food and shelter. Aid organizations, such as Oxfam and Médecins Sans Frontières, supply clean water, food, medicines, and shelter.

Wildfire

Forest fire warning

From the first flicker of flame in dry grass, a wildfire spreads rapidly. Also known as bush fires or forest fires, wildfires regularly occur during the long, dry summers in Australia, California, and southern Europe. Some are left to burn out, and the landscape regenerates naturally. When a wildfire is out of control, firefighters battle to stop it destroying whole forests or spreading to built-up areas.

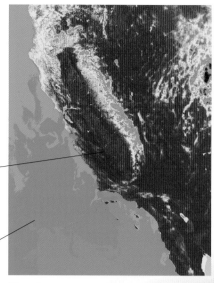

Dark red areas are the hottest, showing ground temperatures above 131°F (55°C)

Cool blue-green area is the Pacific Ocean

Heatwave

This thermal satellite image shows temperatures in California in May 2004, when a heatwave led to an early wildfire season. In hot years, little rain dries out vegetation, making it easier to set alight and harder to stop a wildfire.

Lightning bolt

About half of all wildfires are started by people; the rest start naturally. The spark that lights most natural fires is lightning. Dry plants in summer provide the fuel, and storm winds fan the flames. Within minutes, an area can be transformed.

Thick, choking smoke rises from a land-clearance fire

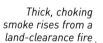

Black Saturday

In early 2009, a series of wildfires struck southeastern Australia, starting on Saturday, February 7, when extremely hot weather and tinder-dry bush sparked blazes. Wildfires occur regularly in Australia, but these were extreme. The intense heat caused firestorms that devoured everything in their path; one firestorm north of Melbourne claimed 120 lives. The fires killed 173 people in total—the worst-ever death toll from wildfire in Australia. The day when they started is now known as Black Saturday.

Farmers' fires

In Southeast Asia and South America, farmers clear rain forest by burning it down. They grow crops on the land for a few years and then let it become forest again. Farmers' fires are difficult to control, and they sometimes grow into dangerous wildfires.

New growth

Wildfires are vital to North American lodgepole pines, which only release seeds in a fire's heat. Forest fires also clear land for new seedlings, return nutrients to soil, and kill pests and diseases.

Indian Ocean

Island of Borneo

Smoke from wildfires

Red dots show fires still burning

An island burns

In the summer of 2002, fires and smoke in Borneo, Southeast Asia, were visible from space. Logging companies started the fires to clear rain forest, but they soon got out of control, destroying an area half the size of Switzerland. Even after a rain forest fire is put out, the peat under the forest smoulders and can reignite flames.

Rising hot air sucks in more air at the bottom, fueling the fire with oxygen

Fighting fires

Cruise speed is 126 mph (203 kph)

It may take a week to bring a wildfire under control. In remote areas, firefighters battle leaping flames, falling trees, choking smoke, and 932°F (500°C) heat. But some wildfires are unstoppable; in 1997, after months of drought, 100 fires blazed in Indonesia's rain forests. Firefighting experts could not bring the fires under control. The monsoon rains finally fell, killing the flames until the next wildfire season.

Helicopter carries one pilot, two fire captains, and eight firefighters

Fire engine
In urban areas, fire engine hoses can connect to fire hydrants for water. In the wilderness, tanks of water are driven to the scene of the fire, or pumped from nearby water sources.

Fighting fires
Firefighters spray water or chemicals onto burning vegetation to lower its heat and make it less flammable. They may cut down or burn vegetation where the fire is heading so that it runs out of fuel. They may also create wide trenches that flames cannot leap over.

Water turned to steam by the heat of the flames

Choking smog
In 1997, raging fires consumed over 300,000 hectares (750,000 acres) of forest in Southeast Asia. The smoke created a gray haze of choking smog that affected 70 million people. Many people wore protective masks in an attempt to try and minimize damage to the lungs.

Health worker hands masks to a commuter

Sparks shoot out as the tree ignites

Flaming tree
Natural oils in Australian *Eucalyptus* trees stop them from drying out in the arid climate, but make them very flammable. In the hot, dry summer, the heat of a nearby fire can make the trees ignite spontaneously. After the fire, new growth can spring from beneath the charred bark, and the fire-resistant seeds germinate in the ash-rich soil.

Tank can hold 360 gallons (1,360 liters) of water or foam

Brightly colored, fire-resistant clothing

Fighting bushfires
Wildfires reached urban areas in New South Wales, Australia, in 2002, destroying 170 homes. Around the bush, firefighters now carry out controlled burnings to clear dry undergrowth and prevent major fires.

High collar protects neck from branches during jump

Dousing the flames
Wildfires are an annual hazard to people living near forested areas of southern California. In 2004, 5,500 fires spread across 168,000 acres (68,000 hectares) of the state. And in 2014, more than 5,500 fires raged across 631,430 acres (255,530 hectares). The local fire service has helicopters that scoop or suck up water from a lake and dump it on the fire or surrounding vegetation to make the area less likely to catch fire.

Smokejumpers
In remote areas, firefighters parachute in to tackle small fires before they spread. They cannot parachute with much, so equipment is dropped separately. Afterward, they often have to hike out of the area carrying the pumps and tools.

Helmet with heavy mesh face mask

Gear

Climate change

Over millions of years, Earth's climate has swung between ice ages and hot periods. Long-term climate change is due to shifts in Earth's tilt, heat from the Sun, and the distance between the Sun and Earth. Earth has been growing warmer for the last 100 years, but the recent rate of change has greatly increased. Most scientists believe this global warming is due to polluting gases from fossil fuels, and that it will probably cause more extreme weather.

Antarctic forests
Earth's climate was very different during the age of dinosaurs; it was a lot warmer than it is today, with trees growing in the Antarctic Circle, providing a habitat for dinosaurs like the small, plant-eating *Leaellynasaura*.

Arctic Sea ice, 1979
One effect of global warming is the reduced sea ice in the Arctic. This satellite image shows the ice sheet that covered Greenland, and sea ice that stretched as far as the north coast of Russia.

Polar habitat under threat
Reduced sea ice threatens the survival of polar bears, because they spend much of their lives traveling across the ice, hunting for seals in the Arctic waters. Warmer conditions in the Arctic may mean that most of the floating ice will become seasonal, melting in summer and reforming in winter.

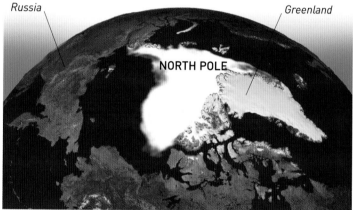

Arctic Sea ice, 2007
This satellite image shows how the summer sea ice shrank in 2007, its all-time low. Scientists think it could melt completely by 2030. The Greenland ice sheet's fringes are thinning, and extra meltwater has raised sea levels, threatening low-lying islands and coasts.

Drifting chunks of ice melt faster than the solid ice sheet

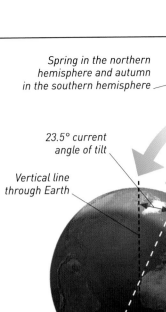

Spring in the northern hemisphere and autumn in the southern hemisphere

23.5° current angle of tilt

Vertical line through Earth

Earth's axis

Earth's orbit changes shape over thousands of years, varying between a circle and an ellipse (oval)

Direction of Earth's spin

Northern hemisphere tilted away from the Sun so it is winter here

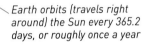

SUN
(not to scale)

Northern hemisphere tilted toward the Sun so it is summer here

Fall in the northern hemisphere and spring in the southern hemisphere

Earth orbits (travels right around) the Sun every 365.2 days, or roughly once a year

Earth's tilt

The seasons are created by Earth's tilt; areas that point toward the Sun receive more heat. This tilt angle changes over many years; the greater the tilt, the greater the seasonal difference. When this coincides with changes in Earth's orbit, taking it closer to or farther from the Sun, its temperature can vary enough to cause an ice age or raise temperatures.

Bleached coral

Rising global temperatures are warming the oceans, threatening tropical coral reefs. A 1.8°F (1°C) rise can make coral eject the plantlike algae that live in their tissues and supply them with food. This makes coral turn white, and ultimately it may die.

Undamaged coral

Bleached coral has no algae

Learning from the past

Geologists drill samples called cores from the ancient ice deep inside the Antarctic ice sheet. These reveal data about surface temperatures over thousands of years, as the ice sheet developed. Ice cores can show how much carbon dioxide, volcanic ash, dust, and pollen used to exist in the atmosphere. Studying how climate and atmosphere have changed may help us predict how it will change in the future.

Hollow drill pipe for extracting ice core

Exploitation

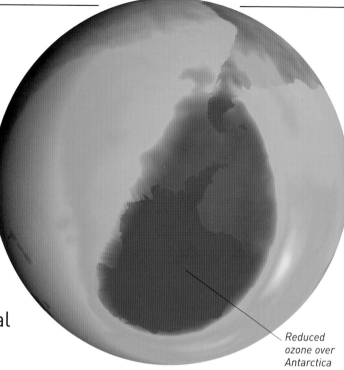

Some disasters are due to our exploitation of nature. Waste fumes from cars or industry pollute the air. Burning fossil fuels provides us with power, but it also releases climate-changing gases. Forests are cut down for lumber and farming; oceans are overfished. Scientists warn that we need to cut our use of natural resources and our production of pollution.

Pollution monitor

Reduced ozone over Antarctica

Thinning ozone

A layer of ozone gas forms in the atmosphere when oxygen reacts with sunlight, blocking some of the Sun's harmful radiation. Gases called CFCs, used in refrigerators and aerosols, react with oxygen and thin the ozone layer, allowing through more of the Sun's rays. CFCs are now banned in many countries.

Redwood forest, northern California

Poisoning the air

Like many cities on hot days, Santiago, Chile, is buried in smog—a sooty fog of harmful gases, including carbon monoxide, produced when vehicle exhaust fumes react with sunlight. The polluted air can aggravate breathing conditions and cause eye irritations.

Deforestation

Forests are being cut down faster than they are replaced. Trees provide lumber, and cleared land can be used for farming. But forests are vital to life on Earth; trees absorb carbon dioxide and produce oxygen. Deforestation can lead to the extinction of species due to the destruction of their habitats.

In China, people flee a duststorm caused by desertification

Desertification
On desert edges, years can go by with little rainfall. When the edges are heavily populated, vegetation is stripped, usually for animal feed, faster than it can grow. Soon desertification, the spread of the desert, turns soil to dust. In Asia and Africa, millions of poor people are losing land and livelihoods as deserts spread.

Catch of herring on a Norwegian trawler

Gray areas show coral damaged by dynamite

Dwindling resources
Factory trawlers like this catch many tons of fish a day. Globally, fish count for 10 percent of our protein intake. As our population grows, so does the demand for fish, and stocks are falling rapidly around the world.

Cutting down a large area of trees can be very harmful to wildlife

Blast fishing
Coral reefs are being damaged by blasting fish out of the water with dynamite. In parts of the developing world, blast fishing is a cheap, quick way to fish, but it kills the coral beneath the waters. It can take more than 20 years before the coral begins to recover.

Acid rain
These trees have been killed by acid rain. Burning fossil fuels releases gases that form acids in the atmosphere. The wind carries the acids far from the places that produced them, until they fall as acid rain, killing trees and poisoning rivers.

Infectious diseases

The world's deadliest disasters are caused by microorganisms—such as bacteria, fungi, and viruses—which invade the body through cuts, food and drink, insect bites, and the air we breathe. They cause infectious diseases—including malaria, cholera, and AIDS—which account for more than 13 million deaths each year. Some can even kill by destroying the crops we depend on for food.

Piercing, sucking mouthparts feed on blood

Deadly flea
In the 14th century, bubonic plague killed 40 million people in Asia and Europe. It was spread by black rats that carried infected fleas. When an infected flea bit a human, its saliva passed on the bacteria that caused the plague.

Long hind legs for jumping between hosts

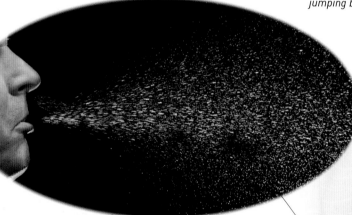

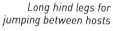

Infectious droplets
Disease-carrying organisms can be spread in water droplets from a sneeze. The common cold, smallpox, and tuberculosis are all spread this way.

Air rushes from the lungs at 93 mph (150 kph)

Rwandan refugees skim a mud puddle for their drinking water

Dirty water
After a disaster, refugees in camps have limited clean water, making cholera a big threat. Caused by bacteria that thrive in dirty water, it causes diarrhea and vomiting, which can lead to severe dehydration.

Power of the microscope
Scientists can study disease-causing microorganisms using microscopes. This scanning electron microscope can magnify objects up to 250,000 times. Dutch scientist Anton van Leeuwenhoek (1632–1723) was the first to observe tiny living organisms such as bacteria under a microscope.

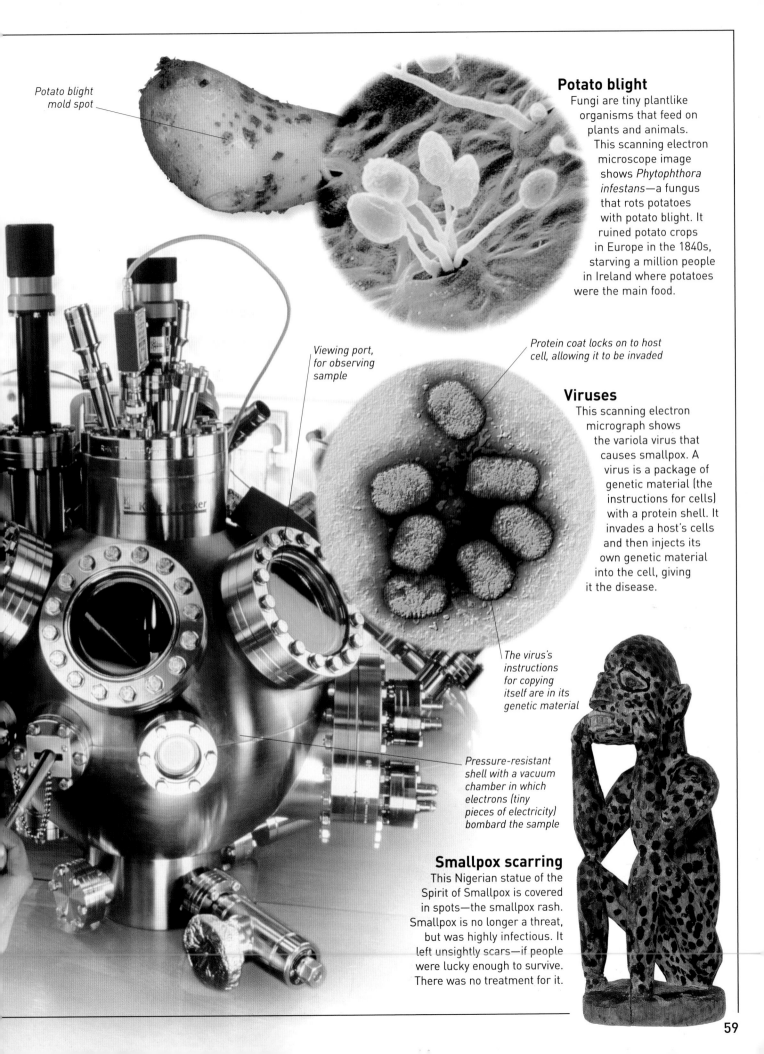

Potato blight mold spot

Potato blight
Fungi are tiny plantlike organisms that feed on plants and animals. This scanning electron microscope image shows *Phytophthora infestans*—a fungus that rots potatoes with potato blight. It ruined potato crops in Europe in the 1840s, starving a million people in Ireland where potatoes were the main food.

Viewing port, for observing sample

Protein coat locks on to host cell, allowing it to be invaded

Viruses
This scanning electron micrograph shows the variola virus that causes smallpox. A virus is a package of genetic material (the instructions for cells) with a protein shell. It invades a host's cells and then injects its own genetic material into the cell, giving it the disease.

The virus's instructions for copying itself are in its genetic material

Pressure-resistant shell with a vacuum chamber in which electrons (tiny pieces of electricity) bombard the sample

Smallpox scarring
This Nigerian statue of the Spirit of Smallpox is covered in spots—the smallpox rash. Smallpox is no longer a threat, but was highly infectious. It left unsightly scars—if people were lucky enough to survive. There was no treatment for it.

Epidemic

A disease that spreads rapidly among people is known as an epidemic. When it affects vast numbers over a wide area, it is a pandemic. In 2014, an Ebola virus outbreak in West Africa looked likely to become a serious threat facing the world. Some epidemics can be averted by killing the disease-carrying organisms, such as mosquitoes; others, by vaccination and health education. Outbreaks of waterborne diseases like cholera can be stopped as long as people have access to clean water.

Flu research

The 1918–20 influenza (flu) pandemic killed 25–50 million people worldwide. Researchers hope to isolate the flu virus from these sample blocks, which contain lung and brain tissue from victims, to discover why this flu strain was so deadly. Flu viruses are hard to treat because they can change form.

Names of victims of the flu pandemic

Vaccinating the world

After two million deaths from smallpox in 1967, the World Health Authority vaccinated everyone at risk, including those in remote areas. A vaccination is a weak form of the disease-causing organism, which stimulates the immune system to build up a resistance. In 1980, smallpox became the only major infectious human disease to be eradicated.

Plague outbreak

In 1994, pneumonic plague—which affects the lungs, but is caused by the same bacteria as glandular bubonic plague—killed 51 in Surat, western India. Street garbage was burned to destroy the disease-carrying rats.

Multi-shot inoculation gun forces vaccine through the skin at high pressure, without a needle

Controlling malaria
The 2004 Asian tsunami left a lot of stagnant water, creating breeding grounds for mosquitoes that could cause malaria outbreaks. In the Bay of Bengal, chemicals were sprayed to kill mosquito larvae.

Mosquito larvae
Mosquito eggs hatch into larvae in water, and then develop into winged adults. Adult females feed on mammal blood, spreading diseases such as malaria and dengue fever. Scientists have not yet found a way to prevent mosquitoes from breeding, so mosquito larvae are killed to help prevent the spread of these diseases.

Infection control
Hygiene is key in the fight against lethal microorganisms, which thrive in dirty conditions. Some, such as MRSA, have grown a resistance to most antibiotics, so treating them is difficult.

Disposable gloves prevent spreading infection

Hospital infection
MRSA (Methicillin-resistant *Staphylococcus aureus*) bacteria can cause a severe infection. Hospital patients with MRSA are isolated to prevent it from spreading, and are treated with powerful antibiotics. In frail patients, MRSA can be fatal.

MRSA bacteria

HIV, colored red, invades a blood cell

HIV and AIDS
The Human Immunodeficiency Virus (HIV), which causes AIDS (Acquired Immune Deficiency Syndrome), kills white blood cells, multiplies, and spreads. As more blood cells are destroyed, the body cannot fight infection. Thirty five million people have HIV, and AIDS is becoming one of the biggest killers in history.

AIDS educators
Candles are lit on World AIDS day for victims, as campaigners try to educate people to prevent its spread. There is no cure for AIDS, and many do not have access to drugs that can control it.

White blood cell, colored green in this image

The future

As Earth's population grows, disasters will cause greater loss of life. The area affected may also be greater. In the future, scientists fear a huge volcanic eruption in the US, and a mega-tsunami from the Canary Islands. In our lifetimes, a global pandemic is a more likely disaster, but a Near Earth Object (NEO) crashing into our planet could wipe out all life in a single blow.

Supervolcano
Below Yellowstone National Park a massive magma chamber heats water that bursts from geysers. If enough pressure built up in the chamber, the resulting volcanic eruption could destroy the US and blast enough ash into the air to cool Earth. Scientists warn that a Yellowstone eruption is overdue.

Killer flu
Diseases that develop strains capable of infecting more than one species can become very potent. The poultry disease, avian influenza (bird flu), infected humans in Hong Kong in 1997. In 2009 in Mexico, swine (pig) flu also infected humans.

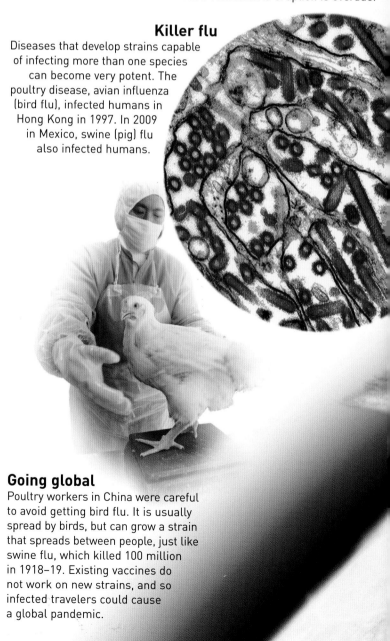

Mount Vesuvius

Devastation of Italy
If Mount Vesuvius exploded today, the effect would be devastating. Southern Italy is the most densely populated high-risk volcanic area on Earth. Naples, which has a million people, would be one of six urban areas in danger.

Going global
Poultry workers in China were careful to avoid getting bird flu. It is usually spread by birds, but can grow a strain that spreads between people, just like swine flu, which killed 100 million in 1918–19. Existing vaccines do not work on new strains, and so infected travelers could cause a global pandemic.

Mega-tsunami
Some scientists think a volcanic eruption could cause half of the Canary Island of La Palma to collapse. The 500-billion-ton landslide would send a mega-tsunami to engulf the east coast of the US with 65-ft- (20-m-) high waves.

First 4 ft (1.2 m) reflecting telescope

Second 4 ft (1.2 m) reflecting telescope

The Cumbre Vieja ridge could collapse

Tracking skies
Optical telescopes, like this twin telescope from Maui Observatory in Hawaii, can track NEOs that could collide with Earth. NASA keeps track of over 12,000 NEOs— none of them heading for Earth just yet. A 0.6-mile- (1-km-) wide NEO would flatten a 300-mile (500-km) area.

Assembly rotates on its base, enabling the two telescopes to track objects

Influenza virus particles shown in red

Culture cells used in virus research shown in blue

Artist's impression of the asteroid or comet strike that destroyed the dinosaurs

Collision course
Evidence suggests that 65 million years ago a 6-mile- (10-km-) wide object hit Mexico's Yucatán Peninsula, producing a mega-tsunami, with waves 0.6 miles (1 km) high. A dust-filled cloud rose into the atmosphere, blocking out the Sun and creating a long global winter. It is thought that this caused the extinction of the dinosaurs and two-thirds of other animal species. To protect Earth from future NEOs, scientists are searching for ways to destroy them, or to push them off course.

Did you know?

AMAZING FACTS

So many volcanoes occur around the Pacific Plate that this zone is known as the Ring of Fire.

The first crater recognized as being created by an asteroid impact was Meteor Crater, Arizona. Before this, people thought it was the remains of an ancient volcano.

Forest fires clear trees and shrubs from the ground, giving the fresh seedlings of California's giant sequoias the space and sunlight they need to grow. The mature sequoia's thick, spongy bark protects the trunk from burning, and its deep roots reach water far underground. It's no wonder some of these trees live to be 3,000 years old.

Burned giant sequoia, California

Rain may fall once in eight years in the Sahara Desert.

Seismograms detect more than a million quakes each year. Only about 150,000 are noticeable.

Tsunamis were once called seismic sea waves, since it was thought they were caused only by earthquakes. Water surface impacts can also trigger them, so the name tsunami, meaning harbor wave, is used.

A tree's inner moisture boils if lightning strikes it, blowing it apart.

Thunder is the sound of air around a bolt of lightning exploding as it is heated to 54,000°F (30,000°C) in less than a second.

For a hurricane to develop over the sea, the sea temperature must be no lower than 80°F (27°C).

In January 1974, a tornado in McComb, Mississippi, threw three buses over a 6-ft- (1.8-m-) high wall.

In December 1952, 4,000 people died in London's coal-driven smog.

From 1550–1850, there were fewer sun spots and solar flares on the Sun, which gave out less heat. On Earth, this was a cooler period called the Little Ice Age.

The 2004 Asian tsunami washed away sand that had buried a 1,200-year-old city at Mahabalipuram, India.

Above Antarctica, the seasonal hole in the ozone layer peaked at 11.3 million sq miles (29.2 million sq km) in 2000. It is getting smaller.

Conditions for drought vary, depending on how much rain is normal and the season. In the US, a drought is

Rain darkens the desert sands

21 days with less than 30 percent normal rainfall; in the Sahara, it is two years without rain.

If out in the open during a tornado, lie down in a low-lying area with your hands over your head until it passes.

The oldest land rocks are 3.5 billion years old; the oldest ocean rocks are just 200 million years old—because new seafloor is added as plates pull apart and old seafloor is subducted elsewhere.

Ozone gas would damage your lungs if breathed, but the ozone layer is vital to filter harmful radiation.

The northern hemisphere has more quakes than the southern.

When the Xiangjiang River, China, flooded homes in

Flooding in Changsha, China

August 2002, some residents in Changsha had to live on a bridge's staircase. The only way people could get around was by boat.

On December 26, 2004, a 10-year-old British girl saw the water recede at Maikhao Beach, Phuket, Thailand. Remembering her school geography lessons, she realized that a tsunami was about to happen. She warned people and saved 100 lives.

QUESTIONS AND ANSWERS

Q How far can lightning travel?

A More than 6 miles (10 km). If a storm is elsewhere, you may still be struck.

Q How are hurricane names decided?

A Each hurricane begins with the next alphabet letter. Male and female names alternate. After a fatal one, the name is dropped. Typhoons are named differently.

Searching for avalanche survivors in Switzerland, 2002

Q How are avalanche survivors found?

A Teams of rescuers probe the snow with long sticks. If it meets an obstruction, they dig to see if someone is buried. Some skiers carry devices that signal to rescuers in an avalanche.

Q What is smog?

A Smog is a mixture of smoke and fog. It is worst when pollutants are in low, cold air under a warmer-air lid. Cities surrounded by hills suffer smog, as low-level air is sheltered from winds and a warm-air lid can settle over it.

Q How did scientists figure out that continents move around Earth?

A In 1915, German scientist Alfred Wegener noticed that the South American continent would fit against Africa's west side. He stated that the continents were once a single landmass. It took 30 years for this to be accepted.

Q What was the world's worst-ever pandemic?

A The 1918–20 influenza epidemic killed 25–50 million worldwide.

Q Is it possible to harness the energy of a volcano?

A In volcanically active countries such as Iceland, geothermal power stations pump water into Earth's crust. Hot magma turns it to steam, which rises and turns turbines for electricity.

Q In which direction do tornadoes spin?

A Tornadoes spin counterclockwise in the northern hemisphere, clockwise in the southern.

Q Why is the weather pattern which switches water currents in the Pacific called El Niño?

A The weather pattern normally occurs around Christmas, and El Niño means "Christ Child" in Spanish.

Erupting volcano

Record Breakers

HEAVIEST HAILSTONES
In 1986, huge hailstones weighing more than 2 lb (1 kg) fell in Gopalganj, Bangladesh.

COUNTRY WITH THE MOST VOLCANOES
Indonesia has the most volcanoes: 130 active volcanoes, and 270 that are dormant or extinct.

MOST EXPENSIVE NATURAL DISASTER
The 2011 Japanese tsunami is the most costly.

WORST RECORDED LIGHTNING STRIKE
In December 1963, lightning struck a plane over Maryland, which crashed killing 81.

FASTEST AVALANCHE
In 1980, Mount St. Helens erupted in the US, triggering a 250-mph (400-kph) avalanche.

Storm waves caused by El Niño strike Malibu, California, in 1983

Timeline

This timeline outlines some of the most devastating natural disasters in history. From the earliest times, scientists and inventors have studied and attempted to predict them. Some of their discoveries are cataloged here, too.

Tyrannosaurus rex fossil (65 MYA)

250 million years ago (MYA) The largest mass extinction in history saw 90 percent of all living organisms die out. Scientists cannot find the cause, but volcanic eruptions in Siberia may have altered the climate worldwide.

65 MYA A massive asteroid or comet hits the Yucatán Peninsula, Mexico, generating a mega-tsunami that plays its part in wiping out two-thirds of all species, including dinosaurs.

c.2200 BCE Records suggest that the city of Troy, in modern Turkey, was hit by a meteor shower that set fire to the city and killed most of its people.

c.1640 BCE The island of Santorini in the Mediterranean erupts, causing a tsunami that destroys the Minoan civilization on Crete. Many people link this event with the legend of Atlantis.

79 CE In Italy, the eruption of Mount Vesuvius destroys the towns of Pompeii and Herculaneum.

132 CE In China, Zhang Heng invents the first earthquake detector.

1348 Black Death, or bubonic plague, arrives in Europe from the East. It kills 40 million people—a quarter of Europe's population.

1441 Concerned about the lives of peasants working the land, King Sejong of Korea orders the development of a rain gauge to forecast floods and droughts.

1492–1900 Ninety percent of Native Americans die, many as a result of infectious diseases, such as smallpox, brought to the continent by Europeans.

1556 On January 3, the most destructive earthquake in recorded history hits Shaanxi province, China, killing 800,000 people. Many of the victims are buried alive.

1703 Edo (now Tokyo), Japan, is destroyed by an earthquake and tsunami which kills 200,000 people.

1752 Dangerous experiments with electricity by Benjamin Franklin will eventually lead to the invention of the lightning conductor.

1755 Triggered by an earthquake, a tsunami hits Lisbon, Portugal, with waves 50 ft (15 m) high and kills 60,000 people.

Minoan palace at Knossos (1640 BCE)

Black Death, London (1348)

1792 An avalanche of debris from the side of Mount Unzen near Nagasaki, Japan, creates a tsunami that kills more than 14,000 people.

1798 English doctor Edward Jenner develops the first vaccine, against smallpox.

Benjamin Franklin's lightning experiment, 1752

1815 Mount Tambora blows apart Sumbawa island, Indonesia, in the largest eruption in recorded history. The dust and gas produced affect the global climate, and 1815 becomes known as the Year Without a Summer.

1840s Potato blight destroys potato crops throughout Europe, bringing widespread famine. In Ireland, most people rely on potatoes for food and more than a million die.

1851–66 China's Yellow and Yangtze rivers flood repeatedly over the land between them known as the Rice Bowl. Up to 50 million people drown.

1860s Weather-observing stations are set up around the globe. Information from a wide area is compared and used for accurate weather forecasts.

1864 Inspired by Swiss philanthropist Henri Dunant, the International Committee of the Red Cross, the first international aid organization, is founded in Geneva, Switzerland.

1874–76 Measles is brought to Fiji, Polynesia, by Europeans and kills one-third of its native people.

1882–83 German scientist Robert Koch identifies the bacteria that cause cholera and tuberculosis.

1883 Eruption of the volcanic island of Krakatau (Krakatoa), Indonesia, causes a tsunami that kills 36,000 people in Java and Sumatra.

1885 British geologist John Milne invents the first modern seismograph for measuring earth tremors.

1900 In the worst local natural disaster in the US's history, a hurricane and storm surge kill more than 6,000 people at Galveston, Texas.

1902 On May 8, Mount Pelée, Martinique, erupts. It leaves only two survivors out of 30,000 in St. Pierre and causes a tsunami in the Caribbean.

1906 The Great San Francisco Earthquake is estimated to have killed nearly 3,000 people. Fires follow and burn the mostly wooden city. New buildings have to conform to quake safety regulations.

1908 A possible comet explodes before impact near Tunguska, in a remote region of northern Russia. The huge blast flattens 850 sq miles (2,200 sq km) of forest, but no deaths are recorded in this largely unpopulated area.

1911 On January 31, on Luzon island in the Philippines, the Ta'al volcano obliterates 13 villages and towns. Most of the 1,335 victims choke on ash and sulfur dioxide.

TransAmerica earthquake-proof skyscraper, San Francisco, 1972

Floods, England, 1953

1917–18 Influenza epidemic kills 20 million people worldwide.

1921–22 A drought and civil war devastate the region of Volga, Russia, causing widespread famine. More than 20 million people are affected.

1923 The Great Kanto Earthquake hits Tokyo, Japan, killing 140,000 people and destroying 360,000 buildings.

1930s Droughts along with poor farming methods lead to the creation of the Dust Bowl across the US states of Kansas, Oklahoma, Texas, Colorado, and New Mexico. Famine forces 300,000 people to abandon their farms.

1931 After heavy rain, the Yangtze River in China rises to 95 ft (29 m) above its normal level, flooding large areas of the country and destroying crops. In the floods and famine that follow, about 3.7 million people die.

1935 American Charles Richter invents the Richter scale to measure earthquake magnitude (size).

1946 Following a tsunami that struck Hawaii, the Pacific Tsunami Warning Center is set up in Honolulu.

1946 The United Nations International Children's Emergency Fund (UNICEF) is founded to provide emergency aid to children in war or a natural disaster.

1953 A storm surge in the North Sea hits the Netherlands with 13-ft (4-m) waves, killing 1,800 people. It also produces 8-ft (2.5-m) waves in Essex, England, killing 300 people.

1958 Lituya Bay, Alaska, is hit by the largest local tsunami in recent history, when a massive landslide produces a wave 1,725 ft (525 m) high.

1960 In May, the largest earthquake ever recorded, measuring 9.5, hits Chile, causing tsunamis that affect Chile, Peru, Hawaii, and Japan.

1968–74 A seven-year drought occurs in the Sahel region of Africa. By 1974, 50 million people are relying on food from international aid agencies.

1970 An earthquake measuring 7.7 occurs off the coast of Peru, causing a massive avalanche and mudslide on the Nevados Huascarán Mountain, which kills 18,000 people.

1971 The worst hurricane (tropical cyclone) in history hits Bangladesh with winds up to 155 mph (250 kph) and a 25-ft (7.5-m) storm surge. The estimated death toll ranges from 300,000 to one million people.

1976 On July 28, an earthquake measuring 7.8 hits Tangshan, China, where 93 percent of the city's mud-brick houses collapse. The earthquake crushes 242,000 people to death.

Krakatau erupts, 1883

1979 After a worldwide vaccination campaign, the WHO announces that it has successfully eradicated smallpox.

1980 On May 18, Mount St. Helens in the US erupts. A successful evacuation is carried out, and only 57 lives are lost.

1984–85 An extended drought in Ethiopia and Sudan in eastern Africa kills 450,000 people.

1985 On November 13, the eruption of Nevado del Ruiz, Colombia, causes a mudslide that covers the town of Armero with 130 ft (40 m) of mud, killing 22,800 people.

1985 An earthquake measuring 8.1 hits Mexico City, killing more than 8,000 people and leaving 30,000 homeless.

1988 In Armenia, an earthquake measuring 6.9 causes newly built apartment buildings to collapse, killing 25,000 people.

1991 Mount Pinatubo, Philippines, erupts in June, ejecting so much debris into the atmosphere that global temperatures drop for 15 months.

1992 In August, Hurricane Andrew strikes the Bahamas, Florida, and Louisiana, killing 65 people and causing $20 billion worth of damage.

1992 In December, a 85-ft- (26-m-) high tsunami hits Flores, Indonesia, killing 2,000 people and making 90,000 homeless.

1993 Summer flooding on the Mississippi and Missouri rivers causes $12 billion worth of damage.

1995 In Kobe, Japan, 5,500 people die as buildings collapse in a 7.2 earthquake.

1997 Pyroclastic flows from Soufrière Hill inundate Plymouth, Montserrat.

1997 In September, wildfires in Indonesia destroy more than 300,000 hectares (741,000 acres) of forest, creating a widespread haze of pollution.

1998 Flooding in Bangladesh caused by a very strong El Niño kills 2,000 people and leaves 30 million homeless.

1998 In October, Hurricane Mitch strikes Central America, killing 11,000 people and leaving 1.5 million homeless.

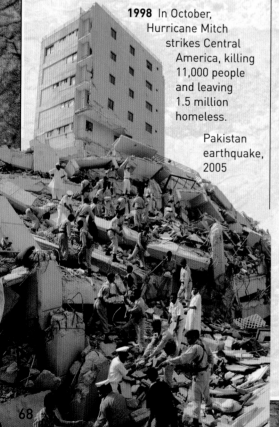

Pakistan earthquake, 2005

1999 On May 3, a tornado outbreak in Oklahoma sees 50 tornadoes rip across the state in one day, killing 40 people.

1999 An earthquake along Turkey's North Anatolian Fault destroys 150,000 buildings in Izmit, killing 17,000 people.

2001 In January, an earthquake in Gujarat, India, flattens 400,000 buildings, killing 20,000 people.

2001 On January 31, huge mudslides caused by an earthquake in El Salvador kill 265 people in the capital, San Salvador.

2002 Severe Acute Respiratory Syndrome (SARS), an unknown viral disease, appears in Guandong, China.

2003 On December 27, an earthquake destroys the city of Bam, Iran, killing 26,000 people.

2004 On December 26, a tsunami in the Indian Ocean kills more than 230,000 people.

2005 In August, category 5 Hurricane Katrina hits the southern US.

2005 On October 8, 86,000 people die in a 7.6 earthquake in northern Pakistan and parts of Kashmir.

2008 Cyclone Nargis strikes Burma (Myanmar) on May 2. Catastrophic floods kill more than 138,000 people.

2008 On May 12, a magnitude 8.0 earthquake kills 68,000 people in Sichuan, China.

2009 The Black Saturday bushfires of February 7 sweep through S.E. Australia.

Tornado, Midwest, US

2010 Up to 100,000 people die in Haiti when an earthquake strikes the most populated part of the country on January 12.

2010 On August 8, heavy rain triggers a mudslide that kills more than 1,470 people in Gansu province, China.

2010–11 Queensland, Australia, suffers a series of crippling floods caused by Cyclone Tasha.

2011 Christchurch, New Zealand, is struck by quakes in February and June.

Health workers, SARS outbreak, 2002

2011 On March 11, a massive earthquake causes a tsunami that devastates the coast of northeast Japan, killing 15,839 people.

2012 Extreme weather plagues the US: a severe heatwave and drought, month-long wildfires in the American West, and Hurricane Sandy, which claims 196 lives.

2013 In November, super-typhoon Haiyan (Yolanda)—the most powerful storm ever to hit land—kills 6,000 people and makes 4 million homeless in the Philippines.

2014 More than 7,000 people are killed across western Africa following an Ebola virus outbreak in March.

Find out more

You can find out more about natural disasters by visiting places mentioned in this book. You could investigate London's Thames Barrier, visit volcanic geysers in Yellowstone National Park, or take a trip back in time to Pompeii, Italy. There is lots of information on the Internet, too.

PLACES TO VISIT

Many large cities have museums that feature in-depth exhibits about Earth's weather, structure, and space. Check your local telephone directory, visit the library, or search the Internet to find out about natural history museums in your area.

Smithsonian Institution
Washington, D.C.
www.si.edu

American Museum of Natural History
New York, New York
www.amnh.org

Field Museum
Chicago, IL
www.fieldmuseum.org

California Academy of Sciences
San Francisco, CA
www.calacademy.org

Yellowstone
The world's first national park owes its creation to its spectacular geological features. Its geysers, hot springs, and bubbling mud are signs of an underground magma chamber.

Yellowstone National Park, founded in 1872

RICHTER SCALE

1	2	3	4	5	6	7	8	9
Recorded on local seismographs, but not generally felt by people			Felt by most; causes little damage	Felt widely; slight damage near epicenter	Large earthquake causes damage to poorly constructed buildings within tens of miles	Major quake, causes serious damage up to 60 miles (100 km) across	Great quake, causing destruction and death for 60 miles (100 km)	Rare great quake causing major damage across 600 miles (1,000 km) or more

The intensity of an earthquake is measured using the Richter scale.

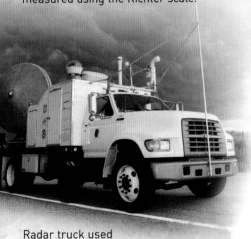

Radar truck used by storm trackers

USEFUL WEBSITES

- **www.geophys.washington.edu/tsunami** follows tsunamis worldwide

- **www.tsunami.org** for the Pacific Tsunami Museum

- **weather.noaa.gov** for the US National Weather Service

- **www.panda.org** for the Worldwide Fund for Nature's infomation on climate change

- **www.weather.yahoo.com** for global weather forecasts

- **www.stormtrack.org** for information about people who track tornadoes

- **www.epa.gov/globalwarming/kids** for global warming info

- **www.who.int** for information on health risks from the World Health Organization

Hurricane scale
The Saffir-Simpson Scale classifies hurricanes by the strength of sustained wind speeds. Short gusts may reach faster speeds. Less than one percent of hurricanes are category 5.

Category	1	2	3	4	5
Description	Weak	Moderate	Strong	Very strong	Devastating
Wind mph (kph)	75–95 (120–153)	96–110 (154–177)	111–130 (178–209)	131–155 (210–249)	156+ (250+)
Storm surge ft (m)	4–5 (1.2–1.5)	6–8 (1.6–2.4)	9–12 (2.5–3.7)	13–18 (3.8–5.5)	18+ (5.5+)
Damage	Minimal: some tree damage	Moderate: major damage to mobile homes and roofs	Extensive: mobile homes destroyed; trees blown down	Extreme: small buildings lose roofs; windows blown in	Catastrophic: roofs of many large buildings lost; storm surges

Glossary

ACID RAIN Rain made more acidic by air pollution from vehicle exhausts and emissions from factories.

AFTERSHOCK A smaller earth tremor after the main shock of an earthquake. Aftershocks may continue for months.

AIR MASS A body of air with a uniform temperature over thousands of miles within the troposphere.

ATMOSPHERE The layer of gases that surrounds Earth.

AVALANCHE A large mass of snow sliding down a mountainside.

BACTERIA (singular, bacterium) Microscopic single-celled organisms that lack a nucleus. Some can cause disease.

BORE A giant wave from an abnormally high tide that rushes up low-lying rivers.

BUOY A float anchored in water, usually to mark a position. Ocean-monitoring devices can be attached to buoys.

CARBON A non-metallic element that occurs in the form of graphite, diamond, and charcoal, and in many compounds.

CLIMATE The regular pattern of weather.

CRATER A bowl-shaped depression at the mouth of a volcano or caused by the impact of a meteorite.

CRUST Earth's thin, rocky outer layer.

CUMULONIMBUS CLOUD A towering white or gray cloud that may bring thunderstorms or hail.

DROUGHT A long period with little or no rainfall.

DUST DEVIL A small twisting wind that lifts dust and debris into the air.

EARTHQUAKE A series of vibrations in Earth's crust, caused by movement at a fault in or between tectonic plates.

EL NIÑO A weather pattern that causes warm water currents in the Pacific Ocean to flow east instead of west. It occurs every few years and can disrupt the weather around the world.

EMBANKMENT A bank of soil or stone, often used to protect an area from floods.

ENVIRONMENT The conditions and surroundings in which something exists.

EPICENTER The point on Earth's surface directly above the focus of an earthquake.

EPIDEMIC An outbreak of a contagious disease that spreads rapidly.

ERUPTION An outpouring of hot gases, lava, and other material from a volcano.

EVACUATION An organized departure of residents from an area.

Crater of Mount Vesuvius, Italy

FAULT A fracture in Earth's crust along which rocks have moved. Transform faults occur in areas where tectonic plates slide past one another.

FLASH FLOOD A flood that occurs suddenly after heavy rain.

FLOOD An overflow of water onto ground that is usually dry.

FLOOD DEFENSES Structures that redirect floodwater to avoid flooding.

FLOOD PLAIN An area of flat land on a river where the river naturally floods.

FOCUS A point within Earth's crust where an earthquake originates.

Aialik Glacier, Alaska

FOSSIL FUEL A fuel such as coal or oil that is derived from the organic remains buried beneath the ground.

FRONT The forward-moving edge of an air mass. A cold front is the leading edge of a cold air mass; a warm front is the leading edge of a warm air mass.

GLACIER A mass of year-round ice and snow that is capable of flowing slowly downhill. The largest glaciers are the Antarctic and Greenland ice sheets.

GLOBAL WARMING A gradual increase in average temperature worldwide.

GROUNDWATER Water that pools in, or flows through, rocks beneath the surface.

HABITAT An organism's natural home.

HAILSTONE A hard pellet of ice that falls from a cumulonimbus thundercloud.

HOT SPOT A site of volcanic activity far from the edges of the tectonic plates caused by magma rising from the mantle.

Lava flowing on Mount Etna, Italy

HURRICANE A violent storm of twisting winds and torrential rain. They are known as cyclones in the Indian Ocean and typhoons in the Pacific Ocean.

ICE AGE A period of time when ice sheets cover a large part of Earth.

IRRIGATION A system of channels for supplying farmland with water.

LANDSLIDE A large mass of rock or soil that slides down a hillside or breaks away from a cliff.

LAVA Molten rock that erupts from a volcano. When underground it is magma.

LEVEE A natural or artificial embankment that prevents a river from overflowing.

LIGHTNING The visible flash during a thunderstorm when electricity is discharged from a cloud.

Rickshaw drivers ride through monsoon floods in Guwahati, India

MAGMA Molten rock beneath Earth's surface. Above the ground, it is lava.

METEORITE A piece of solid material that has traveled from space, through Earth's atmosphere to land on Earth.

METEOROLOGIST A scientist who studies the weather.

MOLTEN Melted to form a hot liquid.

MONSOON A seasonal wind that, when it blows from the southwest, brings heavy summer rains to southern Asia.

OZONE LAYER The layer of gas in the stratosphere that helps protect Earth from the Sun's harmful radiation.

PANDEMIC A disease outbreak that spreads to a vast number of people over a wide area.

PYROCLASTIC FLOW A fast-flowing and destructive outpouring of hot ash, rock, and gases from a volcano.

RADAR A system for detecting distant objects with reflected radio waves to determine size, position, and movement.

RICHTER SCALE A scale used for measuring the intensity of earthquakes.

SAFFIR-SIMPSON SCALE A scale used to measure the intensity of hurricanes.

SATELLITE An object that orbits a planet. Artificial satellites orbit Earth and monitor the weather, ground movements, and changes in sea level.

SEISMIC Caused by an earthquake.

SEISMOGRAM A record of seismic activity on paper or on a computer produced by a seismograph.

SEISMOGRAPH A device for detecting, recording, and measuring earth tremors.

SLUICE A manmade channel with a gate for regulating water flow, used to redirect excess water in order to prevent flooding.

SMOG Fog polluted with smoke.

Supercell cloud

SONAR A system that detects underwater surfaces with reflected sound waves.

STORM SURGE An unusually high tide produced by the eye of a hurricane.

STRATOSPHERE The atmosphere layer above the troposphere, where the ozone layer is found.

SUNSPOT A dark area on the surface of the Sun; magnetic forces hold back light.

SUPERCELL CLOUD A huge storm cloud that may produce a tornado.

TECTONIC PLATE One of about 20 pieces that make up Earth's crust. The parts that carry the continents are denser and thicker than the ocean parts.

THUNDER The sound of air expanding rapidly when it is heated by lightning.

TORNADO A spinning wind that appears as a funnel-shaped cloud reaching down to the ground.

TREMOR A shaking or vibrating movement.

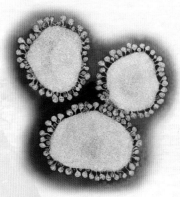

Coronavirus particles

TRIBUTARY A river or stream that flows into a larger one.

TROPOSPHERE The layer of the atmosphere closest to Earth's surface where all weather happens.

TSUNAMI Fast-moving ocean waves, generated by tectonic movements or by an object impacting the water's surface.

VENT An opening in a volcano through which lava or volcanic gases flow.

VIRUS An infectious microscopic package of chemicals in a protein coat. They invade and destroy living cells.

VOLCANO An opening in Earth's crust through which lava escapes.

VOLCANOLOGIST A scientist who studies volcanoes.

VORTEX A spiraling mass of liquid or gas. A tornado's center is a vortex.

WATERSPOUT A tornado over water; a spinning column of mist and spray.

WAVE CREST A wave's highest point.

WAVE TROUGH A wave's lowest point.

Index

ABC

acid rain 57, 70
aftershocks 11, 70
aid organizations 22, 49, 66, 67
AIDS 58, 59, 61, 65
air masses 32, 33, 34, 42, 70
Andrew, Hurricane 38–39, 68
Antarctic 54
Aral Sea 48
Arctic Sea ice 54
ash, volcanic 28, 29, 32, 66
Asian tsunami (2004) 15, 18–19, 22–23, 24, 66, 68
asteroids 14, 16, 17, 62, 63, 66, 67
atmosphere 32–33, 36, 56, 57, 64, 70
avalanches 30, 65, 66
bacteria 58, 60, 67, 70
Bam earthquake 12, 68
bird flu 62
bores 17, 70
boundaries, tectonic 9
buildings, quake-proof 12, 67
Canary Islands 62, 63
CFCs 56
cholera 58, 60, 67
Christchurch earthquake 68
cinder cone volcanoes 27
cliffs 31
climate 32, 70
climate change 54–55, 66
clouds 32, 34, 35, 42
cold, common 58
cones, volcanic 27, 28
continents 8, 65
coral reefs 55, 57
core, Earth's 8
cores, ice 55
crop failures 48, 49, 58, 59
crust, Earth's 8, 9, 26, 70
Cumbre Vieja ridge 63
cyclones 26, 39, 68

DEF

dams 45, 46
debris flows 31
deforestation 50, 51, 56–57
desertification 57
deserts 33, 48
dinosaurs 54, 63, 66
diseases 7, 58–61, 62, 65
dogs 13, 22, 30
Doppler radars 43, 45
dormant volcanoes 26
droughts 7, 48–49, 50, 64, 67, 70
dust bowls 49, 67
dust devils 33
dust storms 33
Earth
  atmosphere 32–33, 70
  climate change 54–55, 66
  natural workings 6, 8–9
  orbit and tilt 55
earthquakes 6, 8, 9, 10–13, 62, 64, 66, 67, 68, 70
  and tsunamis 14–15, 16, 20, 22–23, 24
El Niño 37, 47, 65, 70
epicenters 10, 18, 70
epidemics 60–61, 67, 68, 70
evacuations 7, 12, 21, 28, 40, 41, 47, 50, 64
eyes/eye walls 36, 37
famines 48–49, 66
faults/fault lines 9, 10, 15, 25, 70
fires 12, 17, 50–53
fish stocks 57
flash floods 44, 45, 70
fleas 58
flood defenses 45, 70
flood plains 44, 46, 70
floodgates 24, 45
floods 21, 36, 40–41, 44–47, 66, 67, 68, 70
Floyd, Hurricane 38
foreshocks 11
forest fires 50–53, 64, 68
fossil fuels 54, 56, 57, 64, 70
Fran, Hurricane 37
Franklin, Benjamin 66
frontal wedging 34
fronts (weather) 33, 70
Fukushima power plant 20–21, 22
fulgurites 35
fungi 58, 59
future disasters 62–63

GHI

geologists 55
Georges, Hurricane 39
geothermal energy 65
glaciers 45, 70
global warming 54, 55, 70
Great Kanto earthquake 67
Great Storm of 1987 39
groundwater 48, 70
habitats 54, 70
hailstones 35, 65, 70
Haiti earthquake 10, 68
health education 60, 61
heatwaves 50
helicopters 30, 52–53
HIV 61
hospital infections 61
hot spots 26, 70
humidity 36, 37, 38
hurricane hunters 38
hurricanes 36–41, 64, 65, 67, 68, 69, 70
hygiene 60, 61
ice ages 63, 64, 70
ice cores 55
ice sheets 54, 55
ice storms 33
infections 58–61, 62, 65
influenza 60, 62–63, 67
islands, volcanic 9, 26
isobars 33
Ivan, Hurricane 36

JKL

Japanese tsunami (2011) 20–21, 23, 65, 68
Katrina, Hurricane 40–41, 68
Kilauea volcano 6, 9
Kobe earthquake 12–13, 68
Koch, Robert 67
Krakatau volcano 67
landslides 14, 16, 17, 30–31, 70
lava 6, 9, 26, 27, 70
Leeuwenhoek, Anton van 58
levees 40, 47, 70
lightning 34–35, 50, 64, 65, 70
lightning conductors 34, 66
Lisbon earthquake 6, 66
Lituya Bay tsunami 16, 67
local tsunamis 14, 16, 17

MNO

magma 9, 26, 62, 65, 69, 70
malaria 7, 58, 61
mass extinctions 63, 66
Mauna Kea volcano 27
Mayan civilization 46
Mayon volcano 7
measles 60, 67
mega-tsunamis 62, 63
mesocyclones 42
mesosphere 32
meteorites 14, 70
meteorologists 34, 35, 38, 71
microorganisms 58
microscopes 58–59
Milne, John 67
Minoan civilization 66
Mitch, Hurricane 68
monitoring and predicting
  avalanches 30
  climate change 55
  earthquakes 10, 11, 18, 24
  hurricanes 37, 38–39
  Near Earth Objects 63
  tornadoes 43
  tsunamis 24–25
  volcanic eruptions 27, 28
  weather 33, 34, 35, 45, 66
monsoon 44, 47, 52, 71
mosquitoes 7, 60, 61
Mount Etna 28–29
Mount Fuji 26
Mount Pelée 14, 67
Mount Pinatubo 29, 32, 68
Mount St. Helens 28, 65, 67
Mount Spurr 32
Mount Tambora 66
Mount Vesuvius 29, 62, 66
MRSA 61
mudslides 30, 67, 68
Nargis, Cyclone 39, 68
natural resources 56, 57
Near Earth Objects (NEO) 62, 63
New Orleans floods 40–41
Nile River 44
Noah's ark 46
nuclear disasters 20–21, 22, 23
oceanic plates 9, 15, 20, 64
optical telescopes 63
ozone layer 56, 64, 71

PRS

Pakistan earthquake (2005) 6, 68
pandemics 60, 61, 62, 71
Paricutin volcano 27
plague 58, 60, 64
polar regions 54
pollution 52, 54, 55, 64, 65, 68
Pompeii 29, 62, 66, 69
population 62
potato blight 59, 66
prevailing winds 33
pyroclastic flows 29, 71
radars 11, 43, 71
radiation levels 21, 22, 64
rainclouds 34
rainfall 31, 34, 36, 37, 44, 48, 57, 64
rain forests 50, 51
rats 60
recovery, post-disaster 22–23
refugee camps 22, 49, 58
rescue teams 13, 21, 22–23, 30, 31, 41, 46, 47, 52–53, 65
Richter scale 10, 67, 69, 71
Ring of Fire 64
Rita, Hurricane 41
rivers, flooding 44–47
rockfalls 31
Saffir-Simpson scale 69, 71
Sahara Desert 48, 64
San Andreas Fault 10
San Francisco earthquake (1906) 67
SARS 68
satellites 25, 32, 34, 36, 37, 38, 39, 50, 71
Scarborough cliff fall 31
seismic waves 10, 69
seismograms 18, 71
seismographs 11, 24, 67, 71
shelters, emergency 13, 22, 40
shield cone volcanoes 27
sluices 45, 71
slumping 31
smallpox 58, 59, 60, 66, 67
smog 52, 54, 64, 65, 71
smoke jumpers 53
snow 30
soil 26, 51, 53, 64
soil creep 31
solar flares 64
sonar 25, 71
Soufrière Hills volcano 14
storm chasers 43
storm surges 37, 38, 40, 67, 71
storms 33–43
stratosphere 32
stratovolcanoes 27
Sun 6, 32, 33, 34, 36, 54, 55
sunspots 64, 71
supercell clouds 42, 71
supervolcanoes 62
Surtsey 26
swine flu 62

TU

Ta'al volcano 67
tectonic plates 8–9, 14, 20, 64, 71
tectonic tsunamis 14–15, 16, 17
temperatures 27, 32, 36, 37, 52, 54, 55
Thames Barrier 45, 69
thermal images 50
thermosphere 32
Three Gorges Dam 45, 46
thunder 34, 64, 71
thunderheads 42
thunderstorms/clouds 32, 33, 34–35
tidal bores 17
Tornado Alley 42
tornadoes 42–43, 64, 65, 68, 71
transform faults 9
tropical storms 36, 37
troposphere 32, 71
tsunamis 6, 9, 14–25, 62, 63, 64, 66, 67, 71
tuberculosis 58, 67
twisters 42–43
typhoons 36, 65
unnatural disasters 56–57

VWY

vaccinations 60
Victoria floods (2010) 47
viruses 58, 59, 62–63, 71
volcanoes 6, 7, 8, 9, 14, 26–29, 62, 63, 64, 65, 66, 67, 69, 71
vortex 43, 71
warning systems 24, 25, 30, 37, 45, 67
water
  and disease 58, 60
  supplies 48
waterspouts 43, 71
waves 16, 18, 71
weather 6, 32, 33, 34–43
weather planes 34, 35, 38
wells 48–49
wildfires 50–3, 68
winds 33, 36–43
Yellowstone National Park 26, 62, 69
Yucatan Peninsula meteorite 63, 66

Acknowledgments

Dorling Kindersley would like to thank:
Hazel Beynon for proofreading, Helen Peters for indexing, and Niki Foreman for text editing.

The publisher would like to thank the following for their kind permission to reproduce their photographs:
(Key: a-above; b-below/bottom; c-center; f-far; l-left; r-right; t-top)

1 Science Photo Library: NOAA. 2 Corbis: Jim Reed (br); Roger Ressmeyer (tr). 2 Getty Images: Jimin Lai/AFP (br). 2 Rex Features: HXL (tl). 3 DK Images: Courtesy of Glasgow Museum (tr); Courtesy of the Museo Archeologico Nazionale di Napoli (bl). Photolibrary.com: Warren Faidley/OSF (tl). Science Photo Library: Planetary Visions Ltd (tr); Zephyr (br). 4 www.bridgeman.co.uk: The Great Wave of Kanagawa, from 'Thirty six views of Mount Fuji', c.1831, colour woodblock print (detail) by Hokusai, Katsushika, Tokyo Fuji Art Museum, Tokyo, Japan (bl). Corbis: Dan Lamont (br). DK Images: (tl); Michael Zabe CONACULTA-INAH-MEX. Authorized reproduction by the Instituto Nacional de Antropologia. Rex Features: Masatoshi Okauchi (cr), Science Photo Library: NASA (tl). 5 Corbis: Alfio Scigliano/Sygma. 6 Corbis: Noburu Hashimoto (b). Getty Images: Jim Sugar/Science Faction (tr). Science Photo Library: (tr); Planetary Visions Ltd (tll). 7 Corbis: Frans Lanting (tr). Getty Images: Aaron McCoy/Lonely Planet Images (cl); Andres Hernandez/Getty Images News (b). Science Photo Library: Eye of Science (cr). 8 DK Images: Courtesy of the Natural History Museum, London (tl). 9 Corbis: (cl), (c); Kevin Schafer (cr). Rob Francis 10 www.bridgeman.co.uk: The Great Wave of Kanagawa, from 'Thirty six views of Mount Fuji', c.1831, colour woodblock print (detail) by Hokusai, Katsushika, Tokyo Fuji Art Museum, Tokyo, Japan (tl). Corbis: Academy of Natural Sciences of Philadelphia (tr); Reuters (br). Science Photo Library: Stephen & Donna O'Meara (cl). 11 Corbis: David de la Paz (t). 11 Science Photo Library: Digital Globe, Eurimage (tll); (tr). 12 Corbis: Lloyd Cluff (bl). Science Photo Library: George Bernard (r). 12–13 Tony Friedkin/Sony Pictures Classics/ZUMA. 13 Corbis: AP (b). Empics Ltd: AP (b). Associate Professor Ted Bryant, Associate Dean of Science, University of Wollongong (t). 14 Corbis: Dadang Tri/Reuters (bl). Empics Ltd: AP (br). Rex Features: SIPA (b). 15 Empics Ltd: (cr); Karim Khamzin/AP (b). Panos Pictures: Tim A. Hetherington (cl). Reuters: Amateur Video Grab (t). 16 Corbis: Thomas Thompson/WFP/Handout/Reuters (cr). Getty Images: Jimin Lai/AFP (b). Panos Pictures: Dieter Telemans (t). 16–17 Corbis: Babu/Reuters (b). 17 Corbis: Bazuki Muhammas/Reuters (bl); Yuriko Nakao (tr). Rex Features: RSR (br). 18 Empics Ltd: Wang Xiaochuan/AP (tr). Rex Features: HXL (tl); Nick Cornish (NCH) (t); SS/Keystone USA (KUS) (cl). 18–19 Corbis: Chaiwat Subprasom/Reuters (b). 19 Rex Features: IJO (br); Roy Garner (c). 20–21 Getty Images: JIJI Press / AFP (b). 20 Getty Images: Yasuyoshil Chiba / AFP (tll). NOAA: (tr). 21 Corbis: Tepco / Xinhua Press (tll); Kyodo / Xinhua Press (tr). Getty Images: DigitalGlobe (c); Yomiuri Shimbun / AFP (tr). 20 Getty Images: Getty Images News (b). Panos Pictures: Dean Chapman (tl). Rex Features: Masatoshi Okauchi (t). 21 Corbis: Chaiwat Subprasom/Reuters (r). Empics Ltd: Lucy Pemoni/AP (cr). Getty Images: Getty Images News (c). Science Photo Library: David Ducros (tll); US Geological Survey (b). 22 Corbis: STR / epa (t). 23 Alamy Images: James P. Jones (b). Getty Images: Kazuhiro Nogi / AFP (t). 22 Corbis: Reuters (br). Science Photo Library: Georg Gerster (b). 23 Corbis: Owen Franken (t). DK Images: Science Museum, London (cr). Science Photo Library: NASA (bl); Zephyr (br). 24 Corbis: Kurt Stier (cl); Patrick Robert/Sygma (tr); Ryan Pyle (b). 24–25 Rex Features: Sipa Press (t). 25 Corbis: Andrea Comas/Reuters (br); Michael S. Yamashita (tl). 26 Corbis: Jose Fuste Raga (t). © Michael Holford: (tl). FLPA—Images of Nature: S. Jonasson (bl). 26–27 Science Photo Library: Bernhard Edmaier (b). 27 Corbis: Reuters (bl), (bc). Robert Harding Picture Library: Tony Waltham (br). 32 Alamy Images: Andrew Parker (br). Science Photo Library: Mauro Fermariello (cl). 28 Corbis: Gary Braasch (b); Roger Ressmeyer (t). 28–29 Corbis: Alfio Scigliano/Sygma (bc). 29 www.bridgeman.co.uk: Private Collection, Archives Charmet (t). Corbis: Alberto Garcia (t). DK Images: Courtesy of the Museo Archeologico Nazionale di Napoli (br). Empics Ltd: Itsuo Inouye/AP Photo (t). 30 Corbis: John Van Hasselt (cr); Lowell Georgia (tr); S.P. Gillette (t). Getty Images: Vedros & Associates/The Image Bank (b). Science Photo Library: Mark Clarke (br). 31 Corbis: Jonathan Blair (br); Reuters (bl), (bc). Robert Harding Picture Library: Tony Waltham (br). 32 Alamy Images: Andrew Parker (br). 32–33 Science Photo Library: NASA (b). 33 Corbis: Christopher Morris (bl). US Marine Corps: Gunnery Sgt. Shannon Arledge (br). 34 Science Photo Library: Jean-Loup Charmet (tl). 34–35 Science Photo Library: Kent Wood (c). 35 Corbis: George Hall (t). FLPA—Images of Nature: Jim Reed (fbr). Science Photo Library: Jim Reed (cb); Peter Menzel (c). 36 Corbis: Frances Litman / All Canada Photos (tr). 36 Science Photo Library: Colin Cuthbert (br); Warren Faidley/OSF (b). Science Photo Library: Jim Reed (c); NOAA (b). 38 Corbis: Reuters (b). 37 Photolibrary.com: Warren Faidley/OSF (b); Warren Faidley/OSF (t). Science Photo Library: Chris Sattlberger (t). 38–39 Science Photo Library: NASA/Goddard Space Flight Center (t). 39 Corbis: epa (tr). 39 Empics Ltd: Dave Martin/AP (br). Getty Images: Ed Pritchard/Stone (c). FLPA—Images of Nature: Irwin Thompson/Dallas Morning News (cl); Vincent Laforet/Pool/Reuters (br) 41 Corbis: Irwin Thompson/Dallas Morning News (cl); Ken Cedeno (br); Michael Ainsworth/Dallas Morning News (br). 40–41 Science Photo Library: NOAA (c). 42 Photolibrary.com: Warren Faidley/OSF (c), (bl), (bc), (tr). 43 Photolibrary.com: Warren Faidley/OSF (tr). (c). Science Photo Library: J.G. Golden (cr); Jim Reed (bl); Mary Beth Angelo (tr). 44 Getty Images: AFP (tr). 44–45 Corbis: Reuters (bc). 45 Corbis: Jim Reed (bc); Reuters (tll); Tom Bean (tr). 46 DK Images: Michael Zabe CONACULTA-INAH-MEX. Authorized reproduction by the Instituto Nacional de Antropologia. 46–47 Corbis: Reuters (b). 47 Corbis: Brooks Kraft (tr); Rafiqur Rahman/Reuters (br); Romeo Ranoco/Reuters (c). Magnum: Philip Jones-Griffiths (tll). 47 Getty Images: Scott Barbour (c). 48 Corbis: Despotovic Dusko/Sygma (cl). Magnum: Steve McCurry (bl). Science Photo Library: Novosti Photo Library (tr). 48–49 Corbis: Reuters (cl). 48 Corbis: Dusko Despotovic / Sygma (cl). 49 Corbis: Howard Davies (br). Getty Images: Time Life Pictures (tl). Photolibrary.com: Sarah Puttnam/Index Stock Imagery (tr). 49 Getty Images: John Moore (cr). 50 Corbis: Polypix, Eye Ubiquitous (tl); Stephenie Maze (bl). FLPA—Images of Nature: Ben Van den Brink/Foto Natura (t). Science Photo Library: NASA (tl). 50–51 Corbis: Jonathan Blair (t). 50–51 Getty Images: The AGE / Fairfax Media (b). 51 Corbis: Douglas Faulkner (tl); Ed Kashi (tr). 52 NASA: Paul Lowe (t). 52–53 Corbis: Steven K. Doi/ZUMA. 53 Corbis: Dan Lamont (b). Panos Pictures: Dean Sewell (c). 54 Getty Images: Highlights for Children / Photolibrary (t). 54 Science Photo Library: NASA (cl), (cr). 54–55 Corbis: Hans Strand. 55 Science Photo Library: Alexis Rosenfield (cl); British Antarctic Survey (cl). 56 Science Photo Library: BSIG, M.I.G./BAEZA (bl); David Hay Jones (tl); NASA (tr). 56–57 Getty Images: Steven Wienberg/Photographer's Choice. 57 FLPA—Images of Nature: Norbert Wu/Minden Pictures (cr). Magnum: Jean Gaumy (tl). Still Pictures: W. Ming (tr). 58 Empics Ltd: David Guttenfelder/AP (bl); Jordan Peter/PA (cl). Science Photo Library: John Burbridge tr. 58–59 Science Photo Library: Colin Cuthbert. 59 Science Photo Library: Andrew Syred (tr); Astrid & Hanns-Frieder Michler (tll); Eye of Science (cr). 60 Empics Ltd: John Moore/AP (bl). Eye Ubiquitous: Hutchison (br). Science Photo Library: James King-Holmes (tl). 61 Corbis: Erik de Castro/Reuters (br); Pallava Bagla (t). Science Photo Library: Colin Cuthbert (c); Andy Crump, TDR, WHO (tr); CDC (cl); NIBSC (bc). 62 Corbis: Claro Cortes IV/Reuters (bc); Jeff Vanuga (t); Roger Ressmeyer (br). Science Photo Library: CDC/C. Goldsmith/J. Katz/S. Zaki (cr). 63 Corbis: Roger Ressmeyer (br). Science Photo Library: NASA (tl), (b). 64 Corbis: Reuters (br); Sally A. Morgan, Ecoscene (l); Ted Soqui (tr). 64–65 Science Photo Library: NASA, background. 65 Corbis: Reuters (l); Vinve Streano (br). Science Photo Library: Russell Kightley (t). 66 Corbis: Gianni Dagli Orti (b). The Art Archive (t). 66 Science Photo Library: Mehau Kulyk (t); Photo Researchers (cr). 66–67 Rob Francis: background. 66–67 Getty Images: Fraser Hall/Robert Harding World Imagery (bc). 67 Photolibrary.com: Mary Plage/OSF (cra). Corbis: Bettmann (crb). Science Photo Library: Bettmann (tc). 68 Corbis: Faisal Mahmood/Reuters (bl); Reuters (cr). Science Photo Library: Eric Nguyen/Jim Reed Photography (tr). 68–69 Rob Francis: background. 69 Corbis: Jim Reed (bl). 70 Science Photo Library: Jeremy Bishop (cr). 71 Corbis: Reuters (t). Science Photo Library: Dr Linda Stannard, UCT (cr); Jim Reed (bc).

All other images © Dorling Kindersley.

For further information, see:
www.dkimages.com